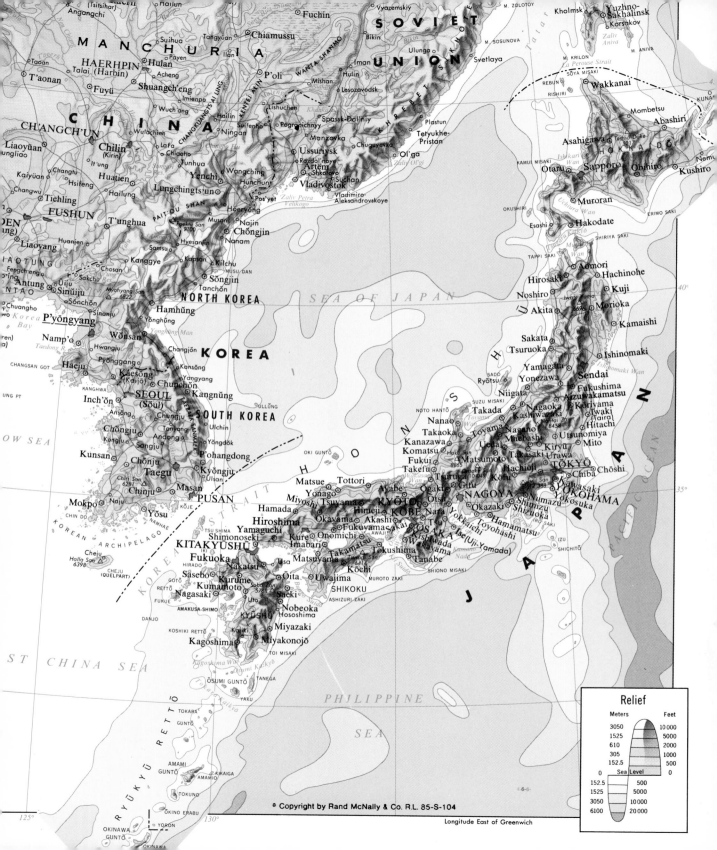

Enchantment of the World

KOREA

By Sylvia McNair

Consultant: Michael Robinson, Ph.D., Assistant Professor of History, University of Southern California, Los Angeles, California

Consultant: Donghee Lee, Assistant Manager, Publication Division, Publicity Department, Korean National Tourism Corporation, Seoul, South Korea

Consultant for Reading: Robert L. Hillerich, Ph.D., Bowling Green State University, Bowling Green, Ohio

CHILDRENS PRESS ®

CHICAGO

Library of Congress Cataloging-in-Publication Data

McNair, Sylvia.
  Korea.

  (Enchantment of the world)
  Includes index.
  Summary: An introduction to the geography, history,
economy, people, culture, and government of The Land of
the Morning Calm, a peninsula dominated by larger
neighbors for many centuries.
  1. Korea—Juvenile literature. [1. Korea] I. Title.
II. Series.
DS902.M35 1986   951.9   85-23273
ISBN 0-516-02771-9

Picture Acknowledgements
AP/Wide World: 31, 48, 49 (2 photos), 51, 54, 74
Cameramann International Ltd.: 4, 5, 9 (2 photos), 11
(left), 29, 30, 34, 36, 52 (bottom left), 57 (right), 58, 60 (top
2 photos), 63 (right), 65, 66, 68 (2 photos), 70 (left), 80, 93,
96 (right), 98 (top and bottom left), 102 (2 photos), 103
(left), 105
Hillstrom Stock Photo: © **Tom Hanley**—Cover (large
photo), 6, 14, 17, 21 (left), 27 (right), 33, 42, 44, 52 (top and
bottom right), 55 (left), 57 (left), 60 (bottom), 72 (right), 82
(left), 85, 87 (right), 88, 98 (bottom right), 106, 108, 110
(left), 111; © **Norma Morrison**—11 (right), 55 (right), 59
(2 photos), 63 (left), 72 (left), 79, 87 (left), 92 (left), 104
(left)
Historical Pictures Service, Chicago: 45, 47, 50
Courtesy Korean National Tourism Corporation: 13, 19
(2 photos), 20 (2 photos), 21 (right), 38 (2 photos), 39
(2 photos), 77 (right), 82 (right), 86 (right), 92 (right), 109,
110 (right)
© **Emilie Lepthien:** 107 (right)
Nawrocki Stock Photo: © **Joel Reznick**—12
© **Chip and Rosa Peterson:** 10 (right), 67, 90, 104 (right)
Photri: 107 (left)
Root Resources: © **John Hoellen**—22, 96 (left), 101
Stock Imagery: Cover (inset), 10 (left), 18, 27 (left), 69
(2 photos), 70 (right), 71, 75, 77 (left), 78, 86 (left)
Third Coast: © **Paul H. Henning**—64, 100, 103 (right)
Maps by Len Meents: 17, 100, 106, 109
Courtesy Flag Research Center, Winchester, MA 01890:
Flags on back cover
Cover: Pusan Harbor/Seoul's Olympic Sports Complex

Guardians at the main gate of Pulguksa Temple

TABLE OF CONTENTS

Chapter 1

THE LAND OF THE MORNING CALM

Korea has been known as "The Land of the Morning Calm" for generations. Its history, however, has almost never been calm.

For centuries the Korean peninsula was dominated by larger, more aggressive neighbors, most often China and Mongolia. From 1910 to 1945 it was occupied by Japan. At the end of World War II it was partitioned into two zones, the north to be administered by the Soviet Union, the south by the United States.

Until then, most people outside of Asia had hardly ever heard of Korea. Even if they knew that it was a country somewhere in Asia, they probably couldn't locate it on a map.

But in the 1950s headlines all over the world suddenly carried news of an invasion of South Korea by troops from the north. The United Nations sent armies to help defend the South Koreans, and a war dragged on for three years. In fact, that war has not yet come to a real end. Actual battles are no longer being fought, but the line between North and South Korea is still defended around the clock by armed guards on both sides.

Even though Korea has been overrun and conquered by outsiders time and again during its more than four thousand years of history, its people have held fast to their own cultural traditions, their own language, their own identity.

And in spite of a most tragic past, this wonderful little country is looking forward to a bright future. That armed border between its two halves is still a sad and frightening thing, but in time it, too, may disappear.

OLD AND NEW KOREA

Life in the big cities of Korea is much like life in any other world capital. People ride to work on buses, subway trains, or bicycles. Modern hotels, huge department stores, tall office buildings of steel and glass fill the downtown areas. Most people wear clothes that would look just as fashionable in New York or Toronto or London as they do in Seoul and Pusan.

After school, Korean children play soccer (or sometimes baseball), watch TV, or play electronic games, just as children do on the opposite side of the world.

Yet the old Korea is still there. It exists in the family loyalty and the respect for elders that is deeply felt by every young Korean. Nothing short of disaster would prevent young Koreans from visiting their grandparents during the three-day New Year's celebration.

It exists in marriage customs. In the old days, matchmakers negotiated a marriage as a business merger between two families; the bride and groom would not even meet until their wedding day. In spite of this, romantic love between husband and wife is a familiar theme in Korean folktales.

Clothing styles reveal Korea's ancient roots and modern outlook.
Left: Young people in Seoul. Right: A traditional wedding ceremony

Today a young man and woman may go out on dates often before marrying, but in some cases, even now, parents have made the selection and arranged the union.

CLOTHING

The old Korea exists in the traditional clothing used for special occasions by all Koreans and for everyday wear by some of the rural people. For women, the colorful attire consists of a long, full skirt *(chima)* gathered to a bodice and topped by a very short jacket *(chogori)* that is tied on one side by a wide strip of cloth in a single bowknot.

The man's traditional costume is white—long pants *(baji)* topped by a sleeveless vest and covered with a long coat called a *turumagi*. The coat is tied in front with a bow like that on the woman's *chogori*.

Left: Man wearing a horsehair hat. Right: Thatched-roof hut in a fishing village

Clothes for dress-up occasions, if the family can afford them, are made of lustrous silk fabric.

Very old men may still wear a topknot—a long braid of hair wound on top of the head—covered by a tall, wide-brimmed, stiff, horsehair hat called a *kat.* These hats were a most prized part of a man's wardrobe. An unmarried man wore the topknot without a hat.

HOUSES OF OLD KOREA

Korean homes were often made of clay, topped by colorful tile roofs of many different intricate designs. Pine shingles, oak bark, flat stones, and thatch made of rice stalks were also used as roofing materials.

Sometimes, when a new house was built and the roof was finished, a couple of tiles would be raised diagonally against each other to form a "good luck gate." The completion of this gate would be the signal for a celebration.

Left: Characteristic Korean architecture
Right: An elegant room in the traditional style

One interesting and very practical invention that has been used for hundreds of years in the design of Korean houses is a type of radiant heating called *ondol*. Traditionally this was heated smoke or air from cooking fires carried through pipes that run under the floors. Today in many homes, the pipes carry heated water. Since people used to sit and sleep on the floor (neither chairs nor beds were common), this heating method suited their needs perfectly.

Inside the houses, sliding walls were made of a special heavy paper. Essential furniture consisted of small tables and chests for holding clothing, bedding, and other possessions.

A kind of antique Korean chest called a *jang* is valuable today. It is typically made of walnut or other decorative wood and lined with cedar. Hammered brass is used for the hinges, lock, and decorative details. These brass fittings, as with many everyday objects in a Korean household, are usually etched with symbols for long life, fertility, and good luck.

THE KOREAN FLAG

Symbols are important throughout Korean art, literature, and tradition. Nowhere is this better illustrated than in the design of the flag of the Republic of Korea (South Korea). This emblem is different from the designs of many national flags of the world in that it is meant to encourage contemplation about the meaning of life and the universe.

In the center of a white background is a circle divided into two parts shaped like intertwined commas. It is called the *taeguk*. The upper half is red, the lower is blue.

The *taeguk* is meant to represent the universe in perfect balance and harmony. The two parts—which the Chinese call *yin* and *yang*—can be interpreted as day and night, good and evil, male and female, heat and cold, or any other opposites that bring existence into balance.

In the four corners of the flag around this center symbol are four different arrangements of black lines in three rows each. The designs are mystical symbols that represent heaven, earth, fire, and water.

Wolchulsan Mountain

THE PEOPLE AND THEIR LAND

Koreans have their own language, despite their history of invasions and occupations by outsiders. The Korean language belongs to the Altaic language family, which also includes Turkish and Mongolian.

Korea is a land with a long history—a history of triumphs, cultural brilliance, and tragedy. It is also a land of people who are courageous in the face of obstacles, steadfast in their loyalties, appreciative of their heritage, and hopeful for the future. As a visitor looks at the mountains all around and watches the early morning mists disappear while the sun rises, Korea's ancient name begins to seem appropriate. It truly is the land of the Morning Calm.

The Songnisan Mountains in central South Korea

Chapter 2

MOUNTAINS, BEACHES,
AND ISLANDS

Korea is a comma-shaped peninsula extending south from China's northeastern corner. A tiny bit of North Korea also borders on Russia and the Siberian city of Vladivostok is only a stone's throw away.

Koreans call the two seas on either side of them the West Sea and the East Sea, but to the Western world they are the Yellow Sea and the Sea of Japan. It is only about 125 miles (201 kilometers) across these seas to Korea's next-door neighbors, China on the west and Japan on the east.

The area of Korea is just a little larger than the state of Idaho and a little smaller than Great Britain. It is about 625 miles (1,006 kilometers) from north to south and 320 miles (515 kilometers) from east to west at its widest point.

Rugged mountains cover about 80 percent of the land of Korea. Not very high when compared with many other mountainous areas, they are nevertheless steep and rocky. Some of the most spectacular mountain scenery in the world can be found on this Asian peninsula. It is said that there is no spot in inland Korea where one cannot look at mountains in every direction.

Korea's highest mountains are in the northern and eastern parts of the land. The highest peak, Mount Paektu on the northern border, is over 9,000 feet (2,743 meters) high. A watershed, a sort of backbone running the length of the peninsula, is formed by the Hamgyongsan Mountains in the north and the Taebaeksan Mountains in the south. This spine is quite close to the east coast. Its slopes drop sharply from jagged peaks toward the Sea of Japan.

The mountains are composed primarily of a very high quality granite. Rocky peaks, narrow canyons, waterfalls, and rushing white-water streams create many beautiful views. In winter they sparkle with a covering of snow and ice.

Most of the eastern shore of Korea is an unbroken thrust of mountains, with sheer cliffs and rocky inlets, but here and there rivers and streams have formed coastal lagoons bordered by sandy beaches at the ocean's edge.

In 1908 an American missionary wrote about the Korean landscape: "As seen from the deck of a ship the Korean coast looks bleak, barren, and generally uninviting. This is just as the natives desired it should look. . . . In order not to tempt outsiders to land and enter their country, the peasants were permitted to cut off all trees and shrubbery from the hillsides facing the sea, thus giving the coast lands a dreary and cheerless appearance not likely to tempt the few passers to care to penetrate into such a forbidding looking land."

Much of Korea's forestland has been destroyed at various times in history, and for different reasons. It may have been true, as the missionary observed, that the trees near the coastline were destroyed during the time of the Hermit Kingdom in order to discourage visitors, but the peasants had even more important reasons for cutting away the woods. They needed fuel for cooking

Transplanting rice seedlings in a South Korean paddy

and to keep warm during the bitter winters. Besides that, land for farming was scarce and valuable in this rocky, hilly countryside, so wherever possible a farmer would clear a forest for crops.

Fortunately, an active campaign to replant pines, oaks, and other trees has been undertaken in recent years to combat the erosion caused by deforestation.

South and west of the main ridge the hills are lower and the slopes more gradual. Rivers course through terraced rice paddies and plains to the Yellow Sea. Rich and fertile deltas are formed by these westward-flowing rivers. Vegetable fields and fruit orchards in this part of the country are a peaceful contrast to the craggy mountains on the horizon.

The Pacific Ocean tides, as they are forced into the West Sea around the tip of the peninsula, are some of the highest in the world. In fact, the tides at the port of Inchon on the west coast are said to be exceeded in height only by the tides of the Bay of Fundy in Canada.

17

Mount Halla on Cheju Island

Korea's many rivers are mainly short, fast flowing, and dotted with sandbars. They are not of much use for transportation, but they are important as a source of water for irrigation and power for the generation of electricity.

Although nearby Japan is famous for its volcanic mountains, Korea has only two volcanic cones, both dormant. One is in the mountains of North Korea, near the Chinese border, and the other is on Cheju Island.

There are numerous islands off the southern and southwestern coasts. Many of these small bits of land are uninhabited, but thousands of cranes, herons, and other waterfowl find refuge there, and the waters teem with fish.

Most picturesque of the islands is Cheju, which used to be known by a Korean name meaning "that place 'way over there."

Mount Halla, 6,397 feet (1,950 meters) high, on Cheju Island, is the tallest peak in the Republic of Korea. Its last volcanic eruption

Left: Cheju's professional divers are women. Right: Autumn foliage

was in A.D. 1007, leaving a large crater and lake near the summit and creating many lava tunnels and pillars.

Tourists like to watch Cheju's professional divers, who are women, harvest shellfish from among the rocks along the coast.

Cheju is Korea's livestock center; there are large grazing lands on the eastern edge of the island.

Korea has a typical temperate climate. But, as in much of East Asia, Korea's climate is affected by seasonal winds called monsoons. There are both winter and summer monsoons, making the winters cold and dry and the summers hot and humid. July, the hottest month, is also the month of heaviest rainfall.

Spring and autumn are pleasant and beautiful. The air is clear, the mountainsides colorful with flowering shrubs in the spring and brilliant foliage in the fall. Many holiday celebrations take place in autumn, after the crops have been harvested. At that time of year, "the sky is high and the horse is fat," a Korean will say.

Korea's climate is favorable for growing a variety of fruits.

Because of the mountainous terrain, great variations in both temperature and rainfall can be found at any given time within the country. For the same reason, the vegetation shows great variety. There are alpine plants at high altitudes, subtropical ones along the southern coast and on the islands. More than 4,500 kinds of plants grow in Korea.

Species of trees range from those familiar to North Americans, such as maple, spruce, elm, pine, birch, poplar, and willow, to more exotic types like bamboo and thuja.

Fruit trees of many kinds find Korea's climate favorable. Orchards yield oranges, tangerines, apples, pears, peaches, apricots, plums, cherries, figs, persimmons, and quinces, as well as walnuts, chestnuts, pine nuts, and ginkgo nuts. Even bananas and pineapples are grown on Cheju Island.

Korean azaleas have been exported widely and are prized in

Left: The tiger, subject of many folk tales and legends, is also a popular subject for artists.
Above: Azaleas at Piwon (Secret Garden) in Seoul

gardens throughout the world. They bloom in profusion on Korea's slopes each spring, along with the flowering fruit trees, lilacs, forsythia, and many varieties of wildflowers.

Bird-watchers enjoy Korea, for several dozen native species and numerous types of migratory birds breed there. Ironically, the demilitarized zone, a strip of land separating North and South Korea, has become a large refuge for many of these migratory birds. Four-footed wildlife in Korea is scarcer today than in former years. And urbanization has driven the remaining animals into remote areas. Tigers, leopards, lynxes, bears, wolves, deer, wild boars, and many smaller mammals are native to Korea.

The land, flora, and fauna of Korea inspired native artists for many centuries. Their paintings, embroidery, and wood carvings depict tigers, deer, and cranes; lotus blossoms and bamboo shoots; rocky cliffs and waterfalls.

The entrance to Pulguksa Temple in Kyongju

Chapter 3

KINGDOMS AND
DYNASTIES

According to legend, Korea was founded in 2333 B.C. A prince had been sent from heaven to govern this peninsula at the edge of East Asia. The prince made his home near a sandalwood tree, not far from a cave where a bear and a tiger lived together. Both animals had a deep desire to become human, so they went to the Heavenly Prince and begged him to give them human form.

The prince gave each animal some garlic and a bitter herb called mugwort. He told them to go back to their cave, stay inside for a hundred days, and eat nothing but the garlic and the herb. If they obeyed his instructions, he would make them human.

The tiger was not patient enough to meet these conditions, but the bear persevered. At the end of the hundred days the prince kept his promise and transformed it into a beautiful woman. Then he made her his queen, and their son was named Tangun, the Sandalwood King.

ANCIENT CHOSON

According to myth, Tangun was the first king in Korea. And if we take the story as fact, his capital established near Pyongyang, which is today the capital of North Korea, would be the oldest capital city in Asia. At that time it was called Choson.

For many years the Korean calendar was computed according to the number of years since the founding of Tangun's kingdom.

Actually, early dates are impossible to verify. Archaeologists have found evidence that the peninsula was inhabited many thousands of years earlier. In any case, it is certain that modern Korean culture has roots that go back more than four thousand years, at the very least.

The first inhabitants of this part of East Asia were probably nomads from the north. The Koreans are believed to share a common racial and language heritage with the Manchus and Mongols, people who live in the northern provinces of China and in the country of Mongolia.

Society in ancient Choson was organized into small clans, or extended family groups, each headed by a patriarch. In those early days before history was written down, decisions probably were made by majority consent. Koreans call this system *hwabaek*.

Clans grew larger and became tribes during the Bronze and Iron Ages. There were frequent wars between tribes all over East Asia. Refugees from the mainland often drifted into Choson.

Boundaries constantly shifted as battles were fought over outposts. In 108 B.C. the Chinese Han dynasty invaded the northwestern part of the peninsula. The conquering Chinese placed the new territory under their control, dividing it into four counties, with its capital at Pyongyang.

This sort of thing has happened over and over again during the last two thousand years. Even though the Koreans are a people quite distinct from the Chinese, they have repeatedly been under the influence of China. But in spite of China's dominance, Koreans still maintained a measure of political independence.

The Chinese called their country the Central, or Middle, Kingdom, meaning that it was the center of all civilization. Korea, in accepting the reality of Chinese power, maintained a special relationship with its northern neighbor. By sending regular missions of respect to China and acknowledging Chinese cultural superiority, the Koreans were generally successful in keeping Chinese political power out of Korea. Yet Koreans continued to borrow Chinese ideas and culture throughout their long history.

One reason for the strength of China's influence was that its written language developed much earlier than Korea's. The system was a complex one, with each character representing an idea, or word. One had to learn thousands of different characters in order to read and write. Because the language was so difficult, only wealthy men of leisure could afford to learn it.

Usually China did not interfere in Korea's internal affairs, but close diplomatic ties were maintained. China kept a close watch on Korea, and Korea paid an annual tribute to China.

THREE KINGDOMS (57 B.C.-A.D. 668)

Around 57 B.C. Chinese control over ancient Choson collapsed for a time, and three native kingdoms were established on the peninsula. All of them were very much under Chinese cultural influence, though their formation brought about a balance of power and stimulated cultural development.

Koguryo, the northern kingdom, included what is now North Korea and part of present-day China, as well. Paekche was in the southwest, among fertile plains and valleys. Silla, the third kingdom, held a small, isolated area along the wild east coast, separated from its neighbors by rugged mountains.

These three kingdoms lasted for the next seven hundred years. During that time the peninsula became primarily an agricultural society, with nomadic tribes in the minority. A powerful and wealthy upper class had developed, supported by taxes collected from the peasants. In Silla there were seventeen ranks of officials. Each level was indicated by the color of robes worn. This hierarchy was called the "bone-rank" system. A person was born into a certain class and could not rise above it.

Even though Chinese influence was still strong, a distinctly separate civilization was developing. As the three kingdoms grew stronger and more stable, they developed codes of law and compiled state histories. Koguryo clashed frequently with Chinese forces, and in the fourth century A.D. there was a conflict between Koguryo and Paekche.

Silla, meanwhile, was building up peaceful relations with China. The combination of Buddhist and Confucian ideas and virtues imported from China was becoming quite popular in Silla. As a result of an alliance between Silla and China, the kingdoms of Koguryo and Paekche were eventually overthrown.

UNIFIED SILLA (668-935)

Once again the Chinese, now governed by the Tang dynasty, tried to set up a suzerainty over the Korean state. But Silla began active resistance to Chinese rule soon after the fall of Koguryo.

Left: A royal crown of the Silla Kingdom. Right: The twenty-three-ton Emille Bell, cast during the Silla dynasty period

Eventually the Chinese were driven out to the north. Silla then ruled over all of the peninsula south of the Taedong River. The area in the extreme north, between the Taedong and Yalu rivers, was not included. This region was not very important, because it is very mountainous and was thinly populated.

So now, for the first time, the peninsula was unified and ruled by a native government. The Unified Silla Kingdom lasted for 267 years and was a great period of Korean culture. In government an elaborate bureaucracy was set up, a system adopted from the Chinese.

The old Silla capital, in Kyongju, was not well located for governing the entire kingdom, as it was in the southeastern section of the peninsula, hard to reach from other parts of the country. But members of the royalty and aristocracy had strong sentimental attachment to Kyongju, so the central capital remained there and five other cities were made subcapitals.

The Silla period was marked by peace, prosperity, and an increase in trade. Foreign trade developed almost accidentally, as part of diplomatic relations between countries. When a representative was sent to another government on an official mission, he would take along many gifts for the rulers. The foreign rulers would, in turn, send other gifts back when the diplomats returned home. Enterprising merchants saw an opportunity to make a profit by piggybacking on this practice. They began to dispatch trade goods along with the gifts. Trade was especially active with China, slightly less so with Japan.

Local markets also developed during this period. Farmers would bring their produce to an area where portable stalls were set up. Each area had a designated regular market day. Trade was conducted through barter. Handcrafted articles were offered, as well as foodstuffs, and each area specialized in the manufacture of a particular product.

Some jewelry and ceramic pieces survive from this period. They show that the Silla artisans achieved a fairly high level of craftsmanship.

The government exercised a strong control over the people. A census was taken every three years, for the purpose of assessing taxes and enforcing military service and corvée labor. Corvée labor was a system of requiring peasants to work for feudal lords for a certain period of time without pay.

The importance of Buddhism in Korea increased greatly during the Silla period. Huge temples were built, many of which still exist and can be visited. There are granite pagodas and statues built of stone, iron, and bronze, dating from the Silla period. Korean monks traveled to China, some even as far as India, to study Buddhist teachings.

Formerly only aristocrats had the privilege of receiving an education.

Education — available only to children of the aristocracy — was based on writings of the Chinese philosopher Confucius. The stated purpose of all education was to train future government officials.

The first school for the training of government workers was established in the year 682. It was called *kukhak,* or National School. A system of examinations at the end of the nine-year training period was used to decide who was eligible to hold public office. However, only members of the royal clan could hold the highest offices.

The Silla period reached its height during the eighth century. It endured for another 150 years after that, but it was on a downhill course. Many things were going wrong. Both the merchant class and the feudal landowners resented strong governmental control. The royal clan was split into rival branches. Confucian officials in lower ranks of the bureaucracy wanted a true merit system for the selection of government officials.

A Confucian ceremony at Chongmyo. Confucian teachings gained a foothold in Korea during the Silla period.

Chinese pirates were sailing the West Sea, robbing the coastal towns and kidnapping their residents. As the power of the landowners grew, the lot of the peasants grew steadily worse, and toward the end of the ninth century large numbers of farmers staged uprisings. Gradually, the Silla government weakened.

KORYO DYNASTY (918-1392)

Three rebel leaders, Kungye, Kyonhwon, and Wang Kon, were directly responsible for the downfall of the Silla government. Each of the three had followers and tried to set up a state. Wang Kon was the successful one. He overthrew Kungye, then Kyonhwon, and was able to reunify the land.

Wang Kon was renamed Taejo ("First King") after his death, and is referred to by that name in Korean history books. He was apparently a wise and good ruler. To encourage the cooperation of

A fresco showing events in the life of Genghis Khan, in his mausoleum in Mongolia

the Silla clan, he appointed the former king to the highest post in his new government. He also married a Silla princess.

The name Koryo, given to the land during the reign of Taejo and his followers, is believed to be a shortened form of Koguryo (one of the former three kingdoms) and a forerunner of the modern name, Korea.

The Koryo dynasty remained in power for nearly five hundred years, but not without many periods of war and invasion. Mongol tribes from the north invaded the peninsula half a dozen times, and the fighting often went on for many years. Troops under the famous Mongol ruler Genghis Khan added Korea to his empire, which stretched across the entire width of Asia.

The Mongols dominated the weakened Koryo state for about a century. They required all crown princes of Koryo to marry Mongols and to live in Peking, China. One of the princes married the daughter of Kublai Khan, grandson of Genghis Khan.

YI DYNASTY (1392-1910)

The next threat to Korean independence came from another direction. Japanese pirates began to raid coastal villages and even make forays into inland settlements. A new Korean leader, General Yi Songgye, drove out the invaders and took over the government in a bloodless coup d'état in 1392.

General Yi was aware that the government was in need of many reforms if it were to last. The most important need was land reform. More and more land had been taken over by powerful landlords during the latter part of the Koryo regime.

Yi asked the Confucian scholar-officials, who held most of the minor government jobs, to draw up a plan. Gradually, they were able to nationalize and redistribute the huge estates.

At the same time Yi managed to reorganize the military, putting an end to private armies. He also deposed the remnants of the Koryo royalty who were still the nominal rulers of the country. In addition, he established close "tributary" relations with the Ming dynasty in China. This brought peace and harmony to foreign relations.

The new dynasty was given the official name of Choson, but it is widely known as the Yi dynasty. It lasted until the Japanese occupation of Korea in 1910.

King Sejong, the fourth ruler of this dynasty, brought about important advances in scholarship, administration, science, medicine, and the humanities. His rule, from 1418 to 1450, was a Golden Age in Korean history.

Sejong encouraged research and gave young scholars government support. He promoted the improvement of printing and devised the idea of creating a phonetic alphabet for the

When King Sejong visited Mount Songni, according to legend, this pine tree lifted its branches for the king to pass. Sejong rewarded the loyal pine by appointing it a minister.

Korean language. The *hangul* alphabet, invented by a committee appointed by Sejong, is simple to learn, phonetically accurate, and a huge achievement for its time.

Sejong was much concerned about the welfare of his people. He provided drought and flood relief for the peasants. Fascinated with science, he encouraged the preparation of a collection of medical books. His reign was marked by comparative peace, and he worked hard toward the goal of an ideal Confucian state.

In spite of the improvements in the lot of some of the people, the social structure of the times was a very rigid one. There were strict class lines, with the royal family at the top of the heap. Beneath them, in order, were the *yangban* (bureaucrats and military officers), *chungin* (minor officials and professionals), *sangin* (commoners, including peasants, fishermen, and merchants), and *ch'onmin* (slaves, serfs, actors, shamans, butchers, and monks). The *ch'onmin* class also included the female entertainers, similar to Japanese *geishas*, known as *kisaeng*.

Wall painting in Pomosa temple, Pusan

Chapter 4

THE HERMIT KINGDOM

Toward the end of the 1500s a powerful and ambitious conqueror, Toyotomi Hideyoshi, was making many sweeping changes in Japan. One of his aims was to conquer China. On his way to the mainland, he intended to take over Korea. He planned to use that country as a military base and draft Koreans into his army to help defeat China.

Hideyoshi had a strong enough army to succeed in a conquest against Korea, but he miscalculated on two counts. For one thing, he did not realize how large Korea was. In the second place, his navy was small and weak.

The Korean navy was far stronger, and if it had gone after the ships carrying Japanese soldiers, the attack could have been stopped before it began. For some strange reason, however, the Korean court simply did not believe the reports they received about the planned invasion.

Yi Sunsin's "turtle ship" sea battle with the Japanese, shown on a plaque beneath his statue

So the Japanese troops landed, captured Pusan, and advanced rapidly northward toward Seoul, the capital. Meeting almost no opposition, they captured first Seoul, then Pyongyang, and drove on toward the Yalu River, the Chinese border.

The Japanese were finally driven back by a combination of Chinese forces and Korean guerrilla troops. At the same time, an even more important action was taking place at sea. A Korean admiral, Yi Sunsin, came up with a brilliant idea. He arranged for iron plates to be fastened to the surface of his junks (ships) in order to protect them from attack.

These ships, called "turtle ships," were in fact the first ironclad vessels in history. They were used successfully nearly three hundred years before the battle between the *Monitor* and the *Merrimac* during the American Civil War. It is hard to understand why, during those three centuries, ironclad ships were never used again by the Koreans, nor copied by any other navies. But they did play a vital part in repelling the Japanese invaders.

The warfare with the Japanese had disastrous effects on Korea. Two-thirds of the country's farmland was left devastated. The Japanese captured and took home with them many of Korea's most capable technicians and artisans. This "brain drain" did much to help Japan progress, especially in the fields of medicine, printing, and the manufacture of ceramics and textiles. On the home front, it left Korea without leadership in those areas.

The state government was seriously weakened, both financially and politically. When the Manchu Empire to the north threatened a takeover of Korea a few years later, they met with little or no resistance. Once again Koreans saw the necessity of acknowledging Chinese "superiority."

POLICY OF ISOLATION

For the next three centuries—the 1600s, 1700s, and 1800s—Korea withdrew from contact with other countries, except for China. Even that contact was limited to regular, formal exchanges of diplomats. Korea was not the only country in Asia to seek isolation. Japan, China, and Burma were also drawing away from contact with other nations.

Besides a natural suspicion of foreign meddling and ideas, which all the Asian countries shared, there was another important reason for Korea's isolationism. The wealthy and powerful landlords, who had had things their way for a long time, realized that international trade and commerce would put money in the pockets of the merchants. In other countries the merchant class was rapidly gaining in wealth and influence. One way to keep the merchants from becoming too important was to discourage any contact with outsiders.

Left: An avenue of stone animals and officers leads up to the tombs of the last two Yi dynasty kings, in Kumkok, outside Seoul. Right: Yi dynasty white porcelain

Also, the Korean attitude in general was very chauvinistic. The people simply could not believe that anything of value could come from any foreign country except China. So while Spanish, Portuguese, Dutch, French, and English adventurers and settlers were sailing the seas and spreading over the entire globe, Korea locked and bolted its doors to outsiders.

The Yi dynasty remained in power until 1910, but Korea after 1600 was more or less at a standstill. It became known as "The Hermit Kingdom." No foreigners were allowed to enter.

Occasionally, a Western ship was wrecked off Korea's shores. In 1628 a Dutch sailor and two of his mates survived a wreck and made their way to Cheju Island. The three were sent to Seoul and not allowed to leave the country.

Twenty-five years later another shipwreck brought a few more Dutch sailors ashore on Cheju. They also were forbidden to leave and remained in Korea for fifteen years. Then they managed to escape and returned to Holland.

The turbulent, rocky waters off Cheju Island were a sailor's nightmare.

One of them, Hendrik Hamel, wrote a book about their experiences in the little-known country of East Asia. Even though this was the first book about Korea ever published in the West, and in spite of the fact that it was translated into English, German, and French, it received little attention.

A few European envoys were sent to the Chinese court in Peking, and from this interchange a trickle of information about the Western world came indirectly to Korea. Some of the Korean diplomats to China were scholars who were genuinely interested in new ideas, especially in science, but their newfound knowledge had little effect on Korean government or society.

As might be expected, without any contact with the rest of the world, ideas and customs became quite stagnant in Korea. In the West this was a period of exploration, new ideas, new experiments in government. In contrast, Korea saw a steady decline in art, literature, and craftsmanship. Even invention, a field in which Korea had excelled, stood still.

CHRISTIANITY COMES TO THE ORIENT

In the eighteenth century a few of the Koreans in Peking became aware of the Western religion of Christianity. Roman Catholic Jesuit missionaries from Portugal were quite influential with the Chinese court. Some of their teachings were carried back to Korea, and the new religion became somewhat popular among farmers and other lower classes.

However, some of the ideas held by the Catholics ran counter to traditional Confucian beliefs. The pope, the head of the Catholic church, forbade ancestor worship, for example. This was frightening to most Koreans, whose regard for family loyalty and devotion was very strong.

In 1785 Roman Catholicism was officially banned in Korea, and the importation of Catholic books was stopped. The early 1800s was a time of severe persecution of Catholics in the Orient. A few French Catholic priests succeeded in getting into Korea, but they were tortured and beheaded. In spite of the dangers, the Catholics claimed a following of more than thirteen thousand Korean converts by the mid-nineteenth century.

In 1866 thousands of Korean Christians were arrested and hundreds were put to death, including some French bishops and priests. In protest, a French diplomat stationed in Peking took matters into his own hands. Without any approval from his own government, he launched a naval attack on Korea. His ship sat at anchor offshore for a time, but left without having any effect on the government's anti-Christian policy.

The United States made several attempts to establish trade with Korea during the 1860s and 1870s. For quite a while Korea held out. But it was impossible for the Hermit Kingdom to stay isolated forever. It was by then the only Asiatic nation without any dealings with the West.

The first crack in the wall appeared with the signing of a treaty of friendship with Japan, in 1876. Six years later Korea and the United States signed a trade agreement. Similar pacts were made with Great Britain, Germany, Italy, Russia, and France. Most of these treaties were drawn up in such a way as to give many more advantages to the foreign powers than to Korea.

At this point, Japan moved in rapidly. Japanese investors set up companies in Korea. Japanese fishermen sailed into Korean waters. Both Japanese and Chinese merchants set up stores for the sale of foreign products in Korea.

The trade was, for the most part, a one-way street. The foreign countries did not buy much from Korea. Because of this, the Korean people were worse off than before.

The next three decades were a time of struggle among Korea's three neighbors, China, Russia, and Japan. Each wanted to control Korea and to prevent the others from putting military bases there. Within the Korean court there were three factions, one pro-Chinese, one pro-Russian, and one pro-Japanese.

Open warfare over Korea broke out in 1894 between Japan and China. Japan was victorious, and China gave up all claim to Korea. For the first time in centuries, little Korea was no longer protected by its "big brother," China. The peace terms said that in the future Japan would act as Korea's protector and would "guarantee" its independence.

Not long after this, Japan again fought over Korea, this time with Russia. Japan was again the victor. After that, other nations no longer interfered with Korea. From 1910 until the end of World War II in 1945, Korea was ruled as a Japanese colony.

The fish market at Pusan harbor

Chapter 5

PERIOD OF MANY CHANGES

The defeat of Russia by Japan in 1905 marked the first time an Asian power had ever overcome a European nation. The main result of this defeat, from the Korean point of view, was the announcement to the world that Korea was now a "protectorate" of Japan.

By 1910 this polite word was scrapped and Japan declared that Korea had been annexed. In other words, Korea as a separate country no longer existed; it was now a possession of Japan.

For the next several decades a Japanese military government in Korea set out to eliminate the Korean culture completely. Two divisions of the Japanese army were stationed in Korea. It was a terrible period in Korean history.

All important government jobs were given to Japanese colonists. Almost all lands owned by the Korean royal family, by the old government, and by the Buddhist temples were confiscated and sold at low prices to Japanese immigrants. Two million Korean farmers were forced off their land.

Japan controlled Korea's fishing industry from 1910 to 1945.

Private fishing was prohibited. Almost all the sardines, crabs, oysters, clams, and other seafood caught in Korean waters was processed by Japanese-owned companies and exported.

A Japanese company, the Oriental Development Company, took over a great deal of property—land, mines, and industry. Trade was carried on exclusively with Japan. Korea's natural resources—iron, magnesium, gold, coal—as well as food and manufactured objects, were exported. In exchange, only cheaply made merchandise from Japan was brought into the country.

Japanese monopolies controlled finance, agriculture, transportation, shipping, industry, fishing, and distribution of goods.

Besides the complete domination of Korea's economic life, the occupation government was harsh and restrictive in all aspects of private and social rights. Civil rights were almost completely wiped out. After 1910, private schools were controlled strictly, and government schools were only gradually opened. Books and magazines in the Korean language were severely controlled.

The Korean ambassador arrives in Japan in 1876.

Korean newspapers were ordered to cease publication. Many editors and writers were put in prison.

Political meetings could be held only with the permission of the military police, who then would stand guard over the meetings. Theaters were carefully watched to be sure that no anti-Japanese propaganda was being voiced.

Police control extended to the areas of public health, butchering, and public conduct. Even more repressive, the Japanese retained, until 1919, the harsh punishment of whipping for misdemeanors. This practice was only for Koreans, not for Japanese residents.

Shinto was the official Japanese religion, and, in the 1930s, worship at Shinto shrines was made mandatory for Koreans.

The two peoples had no respect for one another. The Japanese considered Koreans to be inferior in every way, deserving of scorn and discrimination. Everything uniquely Korean, they felt, should be ignored or wiped out. On the other hand, Koreans thought of the Japanese as tyrants and barbarians, parasites on the cultures of other people, with no real culture of their own.

In 1915 the restrictions on schools were eased. In theory, free education was then available for everyone. Previously only the children of wealthy Koreans had been able to attend school. Actually, though, only about one-third of the Korean youngsters really went to school once the schools were opened to everyone, though nearly all the Japanese children living in Korea did.

Subjects were taught in Japanese, the new "national language." Korean was taught only a few hours a week. By 1938, even the teaching of the Korean language was discontinued. At that time a rule was handed down that seemed almost more cruel than anything that had been done before. All Koreans had to give up their Korean names and adopt Japanese names in their place.

There is no doubt that the Japanese government was heartless and exploitive. It must be mentioned, however, that it did much to improve and modernize the country's material conditions. Roads and rail lines were extended and upgraded, making transportation much easier. Factories and hydroelectric power plants were built, especially in the north.

The north concentrated on industry, the south on agriculture. The result of this specialization was that when the country was divided, at the end of World War II, South Korea suffered from a lack of modern industrial plants and knowledge.

Japanese totalitarianism only made Koreans more intensely proud of their own people, history, culture, and language. They never did think of themselves as Japanese, and never would. Japanese oppression created a strong anti-Japanese sentiment in Korea. And nationalist leaders exploited this feeling in their efforts to overthrow Japanese rule.

These attitudes surfaced in 1919, when thousands of Koreans staged peaceful marches in the name of Korean independence. It is

Japan's Prince Hirobumi Ito (center) and the Korean crown prince (seated).
Ito was assassinated by a Korean in 1909, a year after this picture was taken.

interesting to note that these nonviolent protests took place several years before Gandhi led similar demonstrations in India.

Korean leaders proclaimed a Declaration of Independence on March 1, a day still celebrated as Korean Independence Day. An underground newspaper appeared. Multitudes of people marched, displayed the Korean flag, and shouted *"Mansei! Mansei!"* ("May Korea live ten thousand years!") The Japanese police rushed to disperse the crowd, but as soon as they broke up a demonstration in one area, another would start in another place.

The retaliation was brutal—seven thousand Koreans were killed and over fifty thousand imprisoned. Many villages were destroyed. The oppressive occupational government continued in power until the end of World War II. At the same time, a few Koreans who left the country formed a government-in-exile.

Japanese soldiers in Korea at the end of World War II, hauling a cart of weapons and equipment to a point where they would surrender it to U.S. forces

WORLD WAR II AND AFTERMATH

Matters got even worse, if that were possible, during World War II. Japan used Korea as a factory-arsenal in which to raise food and manufacture goods for the war effort. Korean citizens were drafted into the Japanese army or forced into long hours of labor in factories and on farms.

On December 1, 1943, the United States, China, and the United Kingdom signed the Cairo Declaration, which pledged support for Korean independence. For the first time in many years, Koreans had some hope of eventual freedom and self-determination.

In February of 1945, however, a meeting of the Allied powers at Yalta discussed the possibility of Korea being governed by a multinational trusteeship at the end of the war in the Pacific. The diplomatic talks were not made public at the time, but it turned out later that the United States and the Soviet Union had secretly made an agreement that led to the division of the Korean nation.

Left: American and South Korean troops in a ditch along the Naktong River during the Korean War. Right: Russian troops marching to their barracks in Pyongyang, North Korea, in 1947

The Japanese were expelled from Korea at the end of the war, but the southern part of the country, below the thirty-eighth parallel, was occupied by an American army and the northern zone by a Soviet army. The occupation was meant to be only temporary, but the division still exists.

In 1948 the Republic of Korea was established in the southern sector. U.S. military government forces left the following year, and the Soviet forces also left the north.

For a very short time it looked as if Korea would be allowed to make it on its own. Then, on June 25, 1950, North Korean troops invaded the south. They moved quickly and captured the city of Seoul within three days.

The United Nations sent military assistance to the Republic of Korea, and Communist China came to the aid of North Korea. Peace talks began about a year later, but dragged on for many months. Finally, in 1953, a cease-fire was agreed upon.

Syngman Rhee, first president of the Republic of Korea

MODERN GOVERNMENT

The first independent government of the Republic of Korea (South Korea) was established by a constitution adopted in 1948. Dr. Syngman Rhee, educated in the United States, was elected the first president. Rhee had been active in the independence movement for many years. He helped form Korea's government-in-exile during the years of Japanese occupation. During World War II he headed the Korean Commission based in Washington, D.C., where he lobbied for recognition of Korea as an independent country. When elected, he was a seventy-three year old political conservative. He resigned from office in 1960 in the face of a nationwide, student-led revolution.

Four presidents followed, with various amendments to the original constitution. The 1980 government (called the Fifth Republic) and constitution provided for a president elected to one seven-year term.

A new constitution approved by national referendum in 1987

Thousands of North Koreans in Pyongyang celebrating the socialist May Day festival

came into force in 1988. It provides for a president directly elected by secret ballot for a single five-year term, a State Council of ministers that the president leads and appoints on recommendation of the prime minister, and a unicameral National Assembly of 299 members directly elected for four years. The assembly proposes, approves and rejects all legislation, including the president's nominee for prime minister.

On February 25, 1993, Kim Young Sam was sworn in as South Korea's seventh president. Kim is the nation's first non-military president in over 30 years. He appointed Hwang In Sung, a former general, cabinet minister, and business leader, as prime minister.

The Democratic People's Republic (North Korea) is a Communist state with one-leader rule. Its government strives to stay on good terms with China and Russia, while dealing with other governments.

Since the Korean War the country has been divided. Families were separated with no travel permitted between the two sectors. In 1993 both governments advocated restrictive reunification of families allowing limited travel between the two countries, and progress toward unity.

South Korea's industry has skyrocketed since World War II.

Chapter 6

KOREA TODAY

Change, rapid change, is a way of life for most people in the world today. In a few countries farming is still the main way people make a living. Other countries are just starting to be industrialized. Still others are on the edge of the electronic, or computer, age.

Few people anywhere have seen so much change, so very quickly, as have the people of Korea during the last few decades. They have rushed from the agricultural age through the industrial period, and today are almost as far into the electronic era as any other part of the world.

Even during the Japanese occupation there was a strong, if small, underground independence movement in Korea. Within this school of thought there were two hostile, uncompromising ideas. One was socialist, or communist. The other was nationalist and democratic. After the end of World War II brought liberation, the north went one way, the south another.

Workers at the Patriotic Knitwear Factory in Pyongyang, North Korea

Because North Korea — or the Democratic People's Republic of Korea (DPRK), as the country is officially named — bases its economic and foreign policy on the principle of *chuche* (self-reliance), it remains closed to most of the world. Consequently, little is known of its internal affairs. But we do know that the North Koreans are intensely proud of their system. And they have worked hard in their isolation to develop their economy. They have a system of education for everyone, who must attend school for eleven years. However, their development of some technology lags behind other nations because of their isolation.

In South Korea, or the Republic of Korea (ROK), modern ways of life and Western influences have been accepted readily. No longer does a visitor to Korea see hundreds of men wearing long white coats and stiff black hats.

Left: Traditional silk clothing for sale. Right: Old and new ways mix in the streets of Seoul.

Korea used to be called, sometimes, the land of white-dressed people. Today white is worn by women only for mourning, by men only rarely. Except for a few elderly gentlemen, or for holiday wear, Korean men dress in Western-style, three-piece suits. Children and women wear bright shirts and sweaters atop jeans or skirts.

Lovely Korean silk jackets are brought out of the *jang* (clothes chest) only for special occasions. Even school uniforms are no longer required; youngsters are free to express their individuality in everyday dress.

Time-honored customs for family life are slowly disappearing. The Confucian ideal was "four generations under one roof." Many of today's young couples choose to move away from their parents and establish their own nuclear families.

Young adults still pay great respect and honor to their grandparents and other elders, however. The generations have close ties with one another. Grandparents are often responsible for the daily care of little children, since in many cases both parents have to work outside the home to make ends meet.

THE ECONOMY

The southern half of the Korean peninsula used to be largely rural. Most people living there depended on farming for a livelihood. Almost no goods were produced for export.

Today we need only to read the labels on many items of clothing and other goods for sale in our local stores to see how far South Korea has come in developing both manufacture and export. Shirts, bags, umbrellas, calculators, radios, TVs—the list of items marked "Made in Korea" goes on and on.

But consumer goods represent only a small part of the country's total exports. The major products sold to the outside world by the Republic of Korea are steel and other metals, industrial machinery, and ships. Next in importance are automobiles, electronics, textiles, footwear, plywood, tires, and plastic products.

Products of mining and manufacturing are also exported in great quantities by the DPRK, mostly to the CIS, People's Republic of China, and various nations of Eastern Europe.

The Republic of Korea is changing, at breakneck speed, from an agricultural to an industrial economy. Its population is moving in large numbers away from farms and villages into cities. Seoul is rapidly growing to be one of the world's largest cities. And South Korea looks more toward the Western nations than toward its neighbors for ideas, trade, and military alliances.

Left: Nam Hae chemical plant near Yosu. Right: The Hyundai motor works in Ulsan

The Korean War left terrible destruction in South Korea. Today there is little evidence of that. Cities and towns have been rebuilt. The economy has grown at an incredible rate. Mining, manufacturing, and exports have all increased many times over.

However, there are still severe problems. Low wages and high rates of inflation make finances a struggle for most families. Few people can own their own homes. President Kim pledged that his administration priorities are to reduce corruption, stop a decline in the nation's work ethnic, and deregulate the economy.

In terms of reunification, in 1993 both North and South Korean governments advocated limited travel between the countries.

The monetary system will not be changed until a smooth process can be achieved. This should prevent a monetary collapse that could occur with a sudden reunification of unlike systems.

Land erosion is a serious concern for Korea. Thick forests that once covered mountains were stripped away long ago by farmers who did not know the importance of preserving topsoil. Then, during the

Young trees planted in a small farm village south of Kyongju

Japanese occupation, forests were destroyed to supply lumber to Japan
for construction and shipbuilding. As part of reforestation, Arbor
Day is celebrated each spring, with many tree planting ceremonies.

SAEMAUL UNDONG

A recent movement has helped the people of South Korea to
"pull themselves up by their bootstraps." It is uniquely Korean;
there's nothing like it elsewhere in the world.

Saemaul Undong, which means the New Community Movement,
was started in 1971. Its initial purpose was to help farmers
improve their productivity and their crops. The motto is
"diligence, self-help, and cooperation." Later on the urban people
began to get involved, too.

This is the way it works. Whatever seems to be badly needed in
a village is discussed. The people get together, elect a leader, draw
up their plans, and get organized. The national government

Saemaul Undong *activities: students cleaning a river (left); roadside improvements (right)*

supplies the materials and advice; the local residents do the work. Through these methods, roofs are repaired, roads and bridges are built, community improvements are made. There are new village halls. Agricultural methods have been improved. Factories have been built. Reforestation projects are carried out. Future plans include health and sanitation projects.

Korea has had an especially difficult history. Few countries have had to endure so much in the way of foreign domination, wartime destruction, and political unrest.

Because of this, the late President Park Chung Hee introduced *Saemaul Undong* to help the people forget the tragedies and misfortunes of their past. The program has helped the Koreans to move ahead toward a modern, prosperous, self-confident society. Perhaps most important of all is the way in which it lifted the national morale. The success of *Saemaul Undong* attracted thousands of foreign visitors to come and study its methods and accomplishments.

Korean women have modernized both their clothing and their home-bound roles.

Chapter 7

EVERYDAY LIFE

KOREAN WOMEN TODAY

Life for Korean women in the past was extremely restricted by ancient Confucian ideas. Every girl was expected to marry young and bear many sons. She was supposed to take such good care of her husband that he would live to be at least sixty years of age, an age that had great symbolic importance. Marriages were arranged by matchmakers. This practice is still fairly common in Korea. However, today the young man and woman chosen for each other are often allowed to go through a period of dating and getting to know each other before the wedding.

Upper-class women once spent most of their lives behind the walls of the family home except during evening hours. At that time the men were required to stay off the streets in order to permit the women to call on one another.

Middle-class women were not quite so confined in their movements, but when they did go out they were expected to cover at least part of their faces. This was done by throwing the *chan'got* (cape) over the head. Women of these classes often helped earn the family income by engaging in business.

A picturesque but extremely tiring and difficult chore that used to occupy women for many hours was caring for the gleaming white clothing worn by men. Garments were taken apart at the seams for washing, then soaked and bleached. "Ironing" was done by pounding the silken cloth for hours and hours with two rounded wooden sticks. Then, after all this work, the garments had to be sewn back together.

Rural and lower-class women had still more freedom of movement than the middle class. The other side of the coin was that they had no rights and were accorded no respect.

In one sense, "women's liberation" came to Korea with the nineteenth-century Christian missionaries. But at the end of World War II, thousands of widows and single women suddenly had to support themselves. Many Korean women since then have carved out distinguished careers in business, government, and the professions. More young women are being educated in universities and graduate schools than ever before.

Even though customs are slowly changing, the traditional status of women in Korea is low. An ideal wife is supposed to serve and obey not only her husband but all her older in-laws as well.

Confucianism supports male dominance in society. And Confucian ideals have slowly strengthened over the last four centuries. Thus, ideals favoring separation of the sexes in schools, men's rights in inheritance laws, and the dominance of fathers in the family remain strong.

Left: Three generations of a Korean family on an outing in the park
Right: In some areas, women still wash clothes by hand in streams.

FILIAL PIETY

"Filial piety" is the basis for all relationships in traditional Korean thinking. Of greatest importance is the father-son relationship—the undying devotion of children to their parents.

The Korean family is paramount. Anyone who does anything that goes counter to family duty meets with great disapproval. A person's actions are looked on as the actions of the family.

The patriarch, or father, has the highest responsibility and authority. He holds this position for life, and it is passed on only upon his death, to his oldest son. The father-son relationship is dominant over the husband-wife relationship.

Family ties extend beyond the immediate family to members of the same clan, that is, all those who have the same family name and can trace their ancestors to the same family seat. One cannot marry anyone with the same name and same family seat, even if the relationship is quite distant.

A family ancestral celebration in Taegu

FAMILY OBSERVANCES

An important holiday is the day on which a young son reaches one hundred days of age. A great feast is prepared and many guests are invited to the celebration.

The baby is dressed in fancy clothing and seated behind a table on which various objects are placed. Then his fortune is told on the basis of which object he touches first. If he chooses the piece of yarn he will have a long life. If his choice is the writing brush he will be a great scholar. If he picks a piece of money he will have wealth. And so on.

Another anniversary to be celebrated is a person's sixtieth birthday—presumably because at one time very few people lived to that ripe old age. The birthday is called *Hwan'gap.* Children and grandchildren gather; relatives and friends are invited. The honored elder is dressed in the very best clothing and given a banquet of fine food and drink.

High school students studying English in a language laboratory. South Korean students are required to study English and a second foreign language, such as Japanese, German, French, or Chinese.

As an old person nears death, the family gathers again to observe various ceremonies of mourning. Those still living are responsible for looking after the graves of their ancestors with great diligence. The traditional belief was that a person's prosperity is directly determined by the location of the tomb and the degree of care given to the ancestral burial spot.

EDUCATION

For children, the most important changes in modern Korea have been in the area of education. Koreans, as a specific part of their Confucian heritage, have always valued education very highly. In former times, though, only wealthy families were able to provide schooling for their children.

Today universal, free, compulsory education is available to all children through the sixth grade. As a result, illiteracy has been reduced to about 4 percent of the population.

This student is writing the Korean alphabet.

The education system consists of four stages: the primary, lower secondary, upper secondary, and higher education levels. Korean primary schools are quite formal and strict. Children go to school for five and a half days each week. They are expected to obey their teachers' directives implicitly.

The Korean alphabet is a wonderfully simple phonetic system of writing. The alphabet, called *hangul*, was invented during King Sejong's reign in 1443. In South Korea, some Chinese characters are also used along with the Korean characters.

Chinese characters, much more complex in appearance than Korean, represent single, unique ideas. A word written in Korean letters may have more than one meaning, just as many English words that sound the same have different meanings (hear and here, too and two, see and sea, for example). But a Chinese character, or ideograph, has only one interpretation. Korean

The campus of Seoul National University

children learn a great many Chinese characters—representing Korean words, however—along with the words spelled out in their own alphabet.

In older books, Korean was printed in vertical columns and read from top to bottom, right to left, and back to front of a book. Today most books are printed and read the Western way— horizontally, left to right, and front to back.

After primary school (grades one through six), almost all children go on to a middle school. Tuition is charged for these grades, but the government plans to make middle school education both free and compulsory as soon as possible. Over 90 percent of middle school graduates go on to high school.

The Republic of Korea has more than two hundred two-year and four-year colleges and universities. One of them, Ewha University, is the largest women's university in the world.

Left: Women at the Korean Folk Village playing the traditional women's seesaw game. The players bounce on the seesaw standing up. Right: Young people in a computer shop

RECREATION

After-school life for Korean children is very much like that of children in Western countries. There are many clubs and extra-curricular activities, including sports, music, dramatics, and so on. Youngsters like to watch television, play electronic games, and listen to Western pop music.

Many paintings, calendars, and greeting cards show girls in traditional dress standing in swings or on a seesaw. The popular way to use the seesaw is to bounce one another high up in the air. As one person comes down, hard, on one end of the board, the other flies, higher each time, into the air.

The use of both swings and seesaws by girls supposedly originated in the days when girls were confined inside walled compounds. By swinging or bouncing high enough, they had a chance to get a brief glimpse of the world beyond the walls.

Left: Taekwondo. *Right: Seoul's Sports Complex.*

Hiking, backpacking, and mountain climbing are popular—even more popular among Korean children than they are with American youths. This may be because the mountains are nearby for all Koreans, which is not true for most American city dwellers. Also, public transportation is excellent, easily accessible all over the country, and very safe for young people to use. Groups of children enjoy going off on their own to explore the countryside.

All the internationally popular sports are played in Korea—baseball, soccer, volleyball, basketball, tennis, table tennis, golf, archery, skating, skiing, wrestling, boxing, shooting, and swimming. In 1988 Seoul, Korea hosted the summer Olympic Games. Also popular are an ancient Oriental type of wrestling called *ssirum* and the martial art of *taekwondo*. As the popularity of *taekwondo* has spread, it has taken on the aspect of a world sport with some two thousand Koreans instructing in more than eighty countries.

Left: A shop selling kimchi *jars. Right: Making* kimchi

FOOD

Like every other country in the world, Korea has many festive
dishes for special occasions. Besides dishes of rice and soup, which
are always presented, at least five different side dishes are served,
and in wealthy homes more than fifteen dishes may be offered.

Everyday meals are, however, quite simple. They may consist
only of rice, a soup made with a meat or fish stock, *kimchi*, and
one or two special foods.

Kimchi is Korea's most universal and best-known dish. It is
basically pickled vegetables, but with a strong and, to those not
used to it, unpleasant smell. It is rich in vitamins and a most
important part of the daily diet of all Korean families.

An assortment of Korean foods

Every fall, enough *kimchi* is prepared to last the family through the winter. A rule of thumb is to start with at least fifty heads of cabbage per family member. The cabbages are seasoned with salt and ground-up red-hot peppers, mixed with pickled turnips, radishes, cucumbers, and other vegetables, then stored in huge earthenware jars to ferment for several weeks. The jars are buried in the ground up to their necks.

Meals for special occasions are apt to start with *kujolpan*. Several cooked meats and vegetables are served on a platter, to be rolled up in thin pancakes and popped into the mouth. Sometimes an elaborate array of appetizers is presented in a "nine-part dish." Eight covered trapezoidal boxes are designed to fit around a center octagonal box, forming a larger octagon. These boxes are often made of a lovely lacquerware.

Left: Korean food features a variety of fresh vegetables.
Right: Sumptuous meal in a Korean restaurant

A popular main dish also has its own unique serving pot. *Sinsollo* is a mixture of meat, fish, vegetables, eggs, nuts, and bean curd cooked in a broth, a little like Japanese *sukiyaki*. It is kept bubbling hot until it is served from a brass chafing dish that has a compartment below the food for flaming charcoal.

Koreans enjoy beef, and beef cattle are imported in considerable quantity. After the cattle are brought into the country, they are fattened up, and the slaughtering and processing is done in Korea. *Pulgogi,* strips of marinated beef cooked over charcoal, and *kalbi,* short ribs, are often served.

Vegetables are always cooked lightly and are customarily highly seasoned with peppers, garlic, soy sauce, and sesame-seed oil.

Rich soups and stews include *kalbitang,* made with beef ribs; *saengson chigye,* a fish and vegetable stew; *maeuntang,* a spicy-hot fish soup; and *manduguk,* a meatball soup.

Food is eaten with a spoon and a pair of chopsticks. Small tables for one or two persons are usually used in the home. Normally there is no specific room for eating, so the little tables are carried to wherever people choose to eat.

HOLIDAYS AND FESTIVALS

Koreans love celebrations, and the year is filled with special holidays and festivals. Some have a religious significance, and some commemorate events in the thousands of years of the country's history.

Perhaps the many years of occupation by foreign powers have given Koreans a more intense desire to celebrate their own special historical events and to keep alive as many uniquely Korean traditions as possible.

Koreans reckoned time according to the lunar calendar for thousands of years before the solar calendar was officially adopted. So some holidays are celebrated on dates of the solar calendar, and a few others on the lunar. To a Westerner, it is somewhat complicated!

The first three days of January are set aside for the celebration of the New Year. They are designated national holidays. However, many Koreans still celebrate on the first day of the lunar year, which is close to the same time.

This is an occasion for family reunions and special honoring of parents and grandparents. Holiday foods are served, the younger generations bow to the older ones, and small children are given little gifts. *Sul* (rice wine) and *ttokkuk* (rice dumpling soup) are always served. Children play on seesaws, fly kites, and play traditional games.

On the feast of Hansik, *people offer food to their ancestors at the gravesites and then have a picnic there.*

Around April 5, on the 105th day of the lunar year, is a holiday called *Hansik.* On this day, rites to worship ancestors are observed early in the morning. Time is set aside for carrying food and wine to ancestral graves and making sure the gravesites are neat and tidy. It is often referred to as either Grave Visiting Day or Cold Food Day. The latter name comes from the tradition, in olden days, of not building a fire or making any hot food on this day. Today Koreans dress in colorful traditional costumes and use the holiday for picnics as well as for honoring their dead ancestors.

Buddha's birthday is celebrated on the eighth day of the fourth lunar month, which places it early in May. This national holiday is one of the most important of the year to Korean Buddhists. It is a very colorful celebration, known as the Feast of Lanterns. All across the country lanterns are hung in Buddhist temple courtyards, then carried in parades through the streets at night.

Tano *Day festivities*

May 5 is Children's Day. It is a time for families to honor their children and take them on special excursions. The parks and playgrounds are well used on this holiday.

Tano Day, the fifth day of the fifth lunar month (near the beginning of June), is a major holiday among rural people. It was originally a ritual day for praying for good harvests. People rested from work, dressed in their finest clothes, and feasted as they did on New Year's Day. Special events were held including wrestling matches for men and swinging competitions for women.

June 6 is nationally recognized as Memorial Day, when services are held to commemorate the country's war dead.

June 15, Farmers' Day, is not a national holiday, but it is traditionally observed in rural areas. Farmers get together to help each other with transplanting and weeding the rice fields. Their work is accompanied by lively folk music and dancing.

July 17 is Constitution Day, a national holiday to remember the founding of the Republic of Korea on July 17, 1948. August 15, Liberation Day, is another patriotic commemoration. It memorializes the surrender of Japan to Allied forces in 1945, which freed Korea from thirty-six years of colonization.

Chusok, which falls on the fifteenth day of the eighth lunar month (in early September), is a harvest festival often called Korean Thanksgiving Day. This is a time to wear traditional dress, visit family tombs, play music, and dance in the streets.

October has three national holidays. October 1 is Armed Forces Day, marked with military programs, parades, and air shows. October 3 is called National Foundation Day. Its celebration is an ancient one, recalling the day when the legendary Tangun founded the kingdom of Choson at Pyongyang, in 2333 B.C. And on October 9, *Hangul* Day, memorial ceremonies, including ancient court dances, are held to honor the invention of the Korean alphabet by King Sejong in the fifteenth century.

Also in October is United Nations Day, October 24. This is not a national holiday, but services are held to pay honor to the UN soldiers who died in the Korean War.

And on December 25, Christmas is observed in Korea as it is in much of the rest of the world.

Several other festivals and observances, while not official national holidays, are given regular attention by Koreans.

Twice a year, at the time of the spring and fall equinoxes, ceremonies are held to honor past Confucian scholars. These rites take place at the Confucian Shrine at Sunghyunkwan (Confucian University). Ceremonial bells and other unusual musical instruments are played. Visitors are welcome, and foreign tourists enjoy photographing the colorful activities.

Left: Dressed up for New Year's. Right: The Silla Culture Festival

The Yi dynasty is honored at the ancestral shrine in Seoul each year with special pageants reenacting historic events. The Silla Culture Festival in Kyongju, held in the autumn, lasts three days and is one of the most elaborate and exciting galas of the year. Local commemorative and cultural festivals are annual events in many cities and provinces, including a cherry blossom festival each spring in Chinhae, near Pusan.

At the end of the year Koreans are supposed to put their affairs in order and settle their debts, to be able to welcome in the new year with a clear conscience. One is not supposed to go to sleep on New Year's Eve. In the old days dances were held that night to expel evil spirits.

There are special rules for bowing.

CUSTOMS AND MANNERS

Extreme courtesy has always been a strong part of Korean tradition. It is said that in earlier times Koreans would even avoid walking on a road if they thought they might get in someone else's way. The ancient Chinese spoke of Korea as the "Eastern Land of Courtesy."

Koreans are much more reserved in manner than are Americans and other Westerners. It is not considered proper to show emotions—to laugh loudly, clap one's hands, or behave in any other boisterous manner. To show happiness, a Korean smiles softly or touches another person very gently. To show anger, one simply stares at another person. An apology consists merely of a smile that seems to ask another's forgiveness.

There are set rules about how to behave toward one's elders, though these rules are less rigid than they used to be. The younger person always greets an older person first. When an older person

*In Korea the old
are honored and the
young are prized.*

comes into a room, the younger one kneels and bows at the waist, then stands until given permission to sit.

When handing something to an older person, the younger one should use both hands. The younger person should not sit too close to an elder, should always rise when an older person enters a room, and should never stand looking down on a seated older person. It is also bad manners to touch an older person or to offer to shake hands.

Traditionally, men and women never spoke, or even nodded, to each other on the street. This rule also is fast dying out. Koreans are becoming much more relaxed and informal in behavior, but many still feel that men and women should not act too familiar with each other in public.

Chairs, though rather new, are becoming more common in Korean homes. People used to sit on the floor, and there are proper and improper ways to sit. The most formal and respectful way is to kneel with one's back straight, sitting on the balls of the feet.

Chapter 8

INVENTION AND CREATIVITY

It is well known that China had an advanced civilization in ancient times, back when most of Europe and North America was still populated by primitive tribes. What is not quite so well recognized is the fact that Korea also was sophisticated and advanced in a number of different areas.

Throughout the early years of history, Korea's scholars and scientists came up with a variety of inventions. Some of these were "firsts" in the world. Others, if not first, were at least developed there independently, without any direct knowledge of what was going on elsewhere.

Korea's earliest school on record was *Taehak* (Great Learning), established in A.D. 372. This and *Kukhak* (National School) existed until the late nineteenth century.

Confucian teaching was designed to create men of noble, even perfect, character. It was not concerned with practical education, with training people for professions. Because the emphasis was on human relationships, science was not pursued as enthusiastically as it might have been. In spite of this, early Koreans came up with some dramatic scientific achievements.

Opposite page: The Bell Pavilion in Seoul

Left: The seventh-century Chomsongdae Observatory, also called the Star Tower, is constructed of 365 stones, corresponding to the 365 days of the year. Right: A ceramics artisan

In A.D. 647 an astronomical observatory was built in the ancient Silla capital, Kyongju. Still in existence, it is believed to be the oldest one in the Far East. The movements of stars and planets have been studied and charted in Korea for at least as long as this observatory has been standing, and probably longer.

The cave temple, Sokkuram, was built around A.D. 750. Its ground plan and the projection of its domed ceiling reflect an advanced understanding of mathematics, engineering, and architecture.

Silla period artisans perfected a bronze alloy that was used in making temple bells. Silla bells were famous for the purity of their tone. In 1277 a Korean Buddhist monk invented artificial glass tiles. This invention led to the development of ceramics manufacture.

Perhaps the most outstanding of Korea's early achievements were in the graphic arts—printing and bookmaking. The earliest printing techniques involved carving entire panels on blocks of wood. Woodblocks have been found in Korea that date from the eighth century A.D. and are the oldest known. The making of books in quantity had to wait for the development of movable metal type, so that many impressions could be made.

The invention of this printing method is usually credited, in the Western world, to Johann Gutenberg, of Germany. Actually the Koreans were printing books with metal type about two hundred years before Gutenberg figured out his process. The date claimed for Korea's first movable metal type is 1234.

The government of Korea first started using cast metal type in 1403. King Taejong is quoted as having said at that time, "In order to have a good government, we must read widely." He went on to point out that wood-block printing was too time-consuming and the blocks too easily broken. Therefore he decreed that cast bronze type should be used.

Fifteenth-century inventions in Korea included a spinning wheel and several astronomical instruments. Surveying instruments and devices for keeping calendar records followed. The sundial was invented in 1437. The remains of a fifteenth-century clock are on display on the grounds of the Toksu Palace in Seoul. It indicated not only the time of day but the seasons and the hours when the sun and moon would rise and set.

During the reign of King Sejong (1419-50), a rain gauge was invented. Records of rainfall have been kept faithfully in Korea ever since. These records go back much farther than those in any other part of the world and are an important source of meteorological information.

Korea's most important fifteenth-century development was the invention of *hangul,* the Korean phonetic alphabet. This, along with printing processes of the time, made it possible for anyone to learn to read. Before that, the complexity of learning Chinese characters had meant that only the leisure class could ever hope to read. Of course, these inventions did not mean that education immediately became widespread. But it was a start.

The first encyclopedia produced anywhere was published by Korean scholars in the fifteenth century. A copy of this 112-volume work is in the Library of Congress in Washington, D.C.

Koreans also claim to have had the first icehouses, a suspension bridge built many years before any were built in the West, and the first ironclad warship.

KOREAN ART

Excavations of tombs dating from about the time of Christ have given evidence that early inhabitants of the Korean peninsula had by then developed a number of arts and crafts. Findings have included ceramics, lacquerware, crystal, and gold ornaments.

The earliest known examples of Korean painting are frescoes on the walls of tombs from the Koguryo dynasty. During the Yi dynasty, artists were employed by the court to paint landscapes, portraits, and elaborate decorative screens. Flowers, animals, and birds have always been popular subjects in Korean art, reflecting Koreans' intense love of nature.

A great deal of symbolism went into the choice of objects to be painted. The sun and the moon stood for the king and queen, for example. Cranes were a symbol of happy marriage. Twelve different symbols were used to mean long life.

A protective dragon in the eaves of Popchusa temple

The blue dragon was the symbol of a ruler and was the protector from the east. Even today the Chinese character for "dragon" is often carved at the eastern end of a building. The white tiger protects from the west, and the Chinese character, or a painting of a tiger, is placed at the western end of a home.

Chinese dragons were always depicted with five claws on each paw. Korean dragons, probably in deference to Korea's status as China's "younger brother," had only four claws. So if you wonder whether an Oriental painting of a dragon is Chinese or Korean— count the claws and you'll know!

Korean paintings often had a simple and misty quality, in contrast to the bolder and more elaborate style of the Chinese.

During the seventeenth century arts and letters for the masses became the fashion. In literature, *hangul* was used, making reading available to more people. The art of calligraphy became popular. And at the same time, artists began to paint more realistic pictures, of ordinary people doing ordinary things.

Left: Weaving flowered mats. Right: A celadon wine vessel of the Koryo dynasty

Rich clay deposits have been used in Korea for many centuries in the making of fine pottery and ceramics. Silla pottery was usually dark in color and decorated with shamanistic (magic spirit) symbols.

Koryo artisans invented a method of inlay on pottery, which was then glazed and fired at a high temperature. Their product, called celadon, was highly prized. The finest examples were a gray green with a deep translucent glaze. Antique celadon is priceless, but excellent copies are being made today.

Sericulture, the raising of silkworms for the production of silk fabric, has been an important industry in the Orient since it was discovered, in China, more than four thousand years ago.

The lustrous silk cloth used for traditional Korean "dress-up" clothes is made in many brilliant colors. Its sheen and softness cannot be matched by today's synthetics. Fine embroidery on silk is a skill for which Koreans are famous. Large screens or long scrolls of embroidery work are beautiful examples.

Korea's classical music and dance are many centuries old.

PERFORMING ARTS

Native Korean music used many ancient stringed and wind instruments, plus drums. Confucian and Buddhist rituals were accompanied by ceremonial music, both vocal and instrumental.

Korean folk dancing probably originated in ceremonies of the ancient shamanistic religion. A form of masked dramatic dance has been performed in Korea since the earliest days of Buddhism.

King Sejong, who did so much for the development of science and learning in Korea, was also devoted to music and the dance. He and the later Yi kings actively promoted these arts.

Drama in Korea grew from the same traditions as the dance. Puppet shows were a derivative of the early mask dramas.

Drama courses are taught at Korean universities. There are several little theaters and occasional theater festivals. But movies and TV are much more popular than stage productions.

87

Golden Buddha in Popchusa temple

Chapter 9

RELIGION IN KOREA

ANIMISM AND SHAMANISM

In ancient days, Koreans believed that all things in nature had powerful spirits, or souls. Consequently, they believed that trees, animals, the wind, all natural forces, and all animate and inanimate objects should be treated with respect.

When it was time to gather a harvest or to kill an animal for food, elaborate rites were performed in order to acknowledge the presence of these spirits.

This practice is known today as animism. As these beliefs developed, over many, many years, leaders arose within the society who were called shamans. These leaders acted as intermediaries with the spirits. The shamans could, it was believed, effect cures, avert bad luck, and persuade the spirits not to do any harm.

Small shrines and altars were built by the sides of roadways for the worship of the gods of land and harvest. Sometimes totem poles would be erected.

Shaman and elderly woman professor at Ewha Women's University,
in a ceremony to contact her ancestors

There are still remnants of animism and shamanism in Korea. A few elderly people, especially in the more remote rural areas, hold these beliefs.

Later on Taoism, Buddhism, and Confucianism were brought into Korea from other countries. All of them were readily accepted. All of them had an influence on Korean thought that remains today, even among those people who have adopted other religions. None of these three religious philosophies claimed to be exclusive, so people could continue the practices identified with animism, even if they embraced the newer beliefs.

The early people did not believe in a single Supreme Being, although they did worship Hanul as the Heavenly Prince whose earthly son, Tangun, founded the kingdom of Choson.

TAOISM

Taoism introduced a multitude of gods, none more important than the rest. The chief objective of Taoism was the search for long life and blessings.

The Chinese characters for the words *Su* (long life) and *Pok* (bliss) are still to be found on all kinds of Korean-made articles— carved on wooden objects, etched on brass, embroidered on clothing. These two wishes are directly descended from Taoist beliefs about the purpose of life.

If an elderly Korean were asked today what the most important elements in life are, the answer would be, without hesitation, that they are "Long life, happiness, health, wealth, and having children."

BUDDHISM

Buddhism, as it was originally developed in India, was a simple faith, without any gods. Buddha himself never claimed to be a god. He taught that the aim of life should be to give up all worldly desires and reach a state of "nirvana." Nirvana is a state of ultimate peace and a complete absence of pain, suffering, worry, and the cares of the world.

As Buddhism spread throughout Asia, it became much more elaborate and it divided into many sects. Complex systems of rules, rewards, and punishments evolved, along with a belief in deities, saints, and saviors.

Actually, Buddhism varies to a greater degree from one place and one sect to another than does Christianity, with all its denominations.

Left: Food for offering at temples. Right: A Buddhist religious ceremony

Buddhism came to Korea in the fourth century A.D. It was superimposed on the ancient beliefs without controversy. Many Buddhist temples in Korea have alongside them shrines to a mountain spirit. Usually this spirit is an old man with a pet tiger, and worship of this spirit is directly descended from animism.

In the thirteenth century A.D. the entire body of Buddhist scriptures was carved on wooden blocks so that they could be printed. The task took sixteen years to complete.

This collection of 81,258 panels, called the *Tripitaka Koreana*, still exists. It is on display at the Haeinsa Temple.

Buddhism has remained an important religion in Korea to the present day. It is undergoing a revival among young people, many of whom are working to modernize its practices. They say they want to transform "mountain Buddhism" into "community Buddhism," and "temple-centered Buddhism" into "socially relevant Buddhism."

Confucian ceremonial rite at Chongmyo (Royal Ancestral Shrine) in Seoul. The ancestral tablets of all twenty-seven Yi kings and their queens are housed here. On the first Sunday in May, wine and incense are offered to the royal Yi spirits.

CONFUCIANISM

The philosopher Confucius lived in the sixth century B.C. Because Confucianism has been so widely studied for so many centuries, it is claimed to be the longest-lasting and most influential system of thought ever developed.

Confucianism has never been considered a religion, in the strict sense, but it is a very well developed ethical and moral system. Its intent was to set rules for all relationships within the family and the state so that everyone could live together harmoniously.

To many non-Orientals, Confucianism seems antidemocratic. Its system of order depends on certain roles in which one person accepts the authority of another without question.

There are five basic relationships, according to Confucius: ruler and subject, father and son, husband and wife, older and younger brother, and friend and friend.

Only the friend-to-friend relationship is one of two equals. The other four are that of superior and inferior. When one accepts these relationships, then the various duties—reverence for ancestors, filial piety, obedience of wife to husband and subject to king, and loyalty to friends—become rules for living.

Confucianism also reveres scholarship and the appreciation of the arts. No supernatural being exists in Confucian teaching.

Koreans accepted Confucianism eagerly and strictly during the early years of the Yi dynasty. They became so devoted in following Confucian teachings that the Chinese, who had taught the beliefs to the Koreans in the first place, gave Koreans credit for being more virtuous than they themselves were.

An important part of Confucian teaching was that the state should be run by a meritocracy. That is, only those people who had studied the science of government and could demonstrate their merit through the passing of examinations should hold important government positions.

Although the Koreans were devoted Confucianists, their system of choosing government officials remained mixed. Inherited aristocratic status continued to play an important role in becoming an official. The class of government officials who actually ran things was called *yangban*.

Rites honoring Confucius are still held each spring and fall.

CHRISTIANITY

The first Koreans to hear about Christianity were diplomatic envoys who were sent to Peking in the seventeenth century. There they met French Jesuit missionaries and were baptized. In the eighteenth century Catholicism enjoyed some popularity among some Yanghan families. The first priest crossed the border into Korea secretly in 1785 and began baptizing believers and ordaining clergy. But persecution of Christians became so severe that the missionaries surrendered to authorities in an attempt to stop it. They were tortured and beheaded in 1839.

An English Protestant missionary sailed up the Taedong River in 1866. He too met with death.

After Korea opened its doors and signed trade agreements with Western countries, in the 1880s, American Protestant missionaries were given permission to enter the country. They were not to preach about their religion but were allowed to open schools and hospitals.

A dramatic event occurred in December 1884 that did much to help the image of the missionaries in the eyes of the king and queen of Korea. During a banquet at the Changdok Palace to celebrate the opening of a new government postal system, a group of young Koreans attempted a coup. During the battle Prince Min was dangerously wounded. Dr. Horace Allen, an American Presbyterian missionary, saved the life of the young prince.

Fighting went on sporadically for several months, and Dr. Allen took care of quite a few wounded victims.

The king and queen, grateful for these services, gave the doctor permission to open a government hospital. They provided the building and funds to run the hospital. Dr. Allen, on salary from his mission board at home, received no compensation from the Koreans.

Other missionaries, both Protestant and Catholic, began to enter Korea in greater numbers. While their early efforts were in the fields of medicine and education, they also quietly spread their ideas about God and religion among the native people.

Left: Ginseng root for sale. Ginseng has been a major herbal medicine for centuries. Believed to be a "cure-all" and to promote longevity, it actually may retard aging. Right: Christian churches by Seoul's east gate

RELIGION IN KOREA TODAY

Today there is complete freedom of worship in South Korea. In North Korea, religious groups are still in existence, although it appears that the present government actively discourages all forms of religious observance.

In South Korea there are about eleven million Buddhists, more than five million followers of Confucianism, a million and a half Catholics, and nearly eight million Protestants.

The Muslim religion was the most recent one to be introduced in Korea, brought by Turkish soldiers who were part of the United Nations forces that took part in the Korean War. There are several thousand Muslims in the country now, and there are Muslim mosques in Seoul, Pusan, and Kwangju.

In addition to these major world religions, there are also religions that mix elements of Christianity with native beliefs. The largest is the *Ch'ondogyo,* the Heavenly Way. Another, *Taejonggyo,* still worships the ancient god Hanul.

Another element of Korean thought, still widely believed in today, is geomancy. It is a system of deciding where and how a house, public building, or grave should be situated. Geomancy became an important belief in Korea toward the end of the Silla period.

The belief is that the configuration of any landscape has an effect on what happens to the people living (or buried) there. Some scholars say that the science of geography is directly descended from geomancy.

Until Christianity came to Korea, none of the religions and beliefs held by Koreans had been exclusive. That is, none had taught that there is only one God and only one true religion.

One could be a Buddhist without giving up spirit worship, or animism. Or one could follow the teachings of Confucius without renouncing Buddhism.

The Korean tradition is one of synthesis, of taking the best from here and there and finding a way of putting it all together.

Belief in the superiority of their own land and of this life over any other shows up in many legends. There are several stories of women who descended from heaven to marry earth-men and live happily as humans. Others tell of animals who above all wanted the happiness of becoming human.

Koreans have always extolled the virtues of longevity, or long life. The hero idealized in much literature and art is the hermit who lies deep in the mountains, eating only the medicinal herbs that assure a long life.

Remember the Chinese ideographs for *Su* and *Pok* that are engraved, printed, or embroidered on many Korean objects—*Su* meaning long life and *Pok* meaning bliss. Longevity is without question the most important blessing anyone can have.

Above: Seoul's modern downtown skyline. Below: Mountains and forests of Songnisan National Park (right). Seoul's capitol building and a sign welcoming Pope John Paul II on his 1984 visit (left)

Chapter 10

ANCIENT TEMPLES, MODERN CITIES

Ancient Koreans believed a mountain to be a meeting place between heaven and earth. There are more than three thousand peaks on the peninsula.

It is possible to see much of the high country by car or bus. But real mountain lovers, whether they are Korean or foreign, prize these areas for hiking and mountain climbing. The Korean-American Mountain Hiking Club organizes weekend trips.

Korea has at least fourteen national parks, most of which are mountainous. There are campgrounds, motels, and villas for overnight.

Mount Sorak National Park, in the extreme northeast section of the Republic of Korea, has been called the "Switzerland of Asia" because of its lovely scenery. Photographers love its waterfalls, rock formations, and hot springs.

Dozens of Buddhist art treasures are located in Mount Chiri National Park. This was the first area to be declared a national park by the government (in 1966), and it is on the highest range of the southern half of the peninsula. Mount Chiri is called the nation's foremost sacred mountain. Ancient people believed that it was inhabited by spirits and goddesses.

A legend told in art on a Seoul temple wall

North Korea is even more mountainous and rugged than South Korea. The wild and rugged Hamgyongsan Mountains, near the east coast, are particularly beautiful. Koreans used to claim that these particular peaks had been given by the gods to their country as a special mark of approval. They are dotted with Buddhist monasteries and were in ancient times places of pilgrimage. Bears, deer, and other wildlife are numerous.

These mountains and the beaches at Wonsan on the east coast and Sorai on the west were greatly loved for their beauty by the American missionaries who lived in North Korea before their evacuation from the country in 1940.

TEMPLES

Korea's Buddhist temples are sure to appear on any world traveler's list of outstanding sight-seeing treats. The decor is not only striking for artistic excellence and exotic use of colors and

A dragonlike fish hanging from the ceiling of Pulguksa temple

materials, but it also reflects a sense of humor and whimsy that is
typical of much Korean art. The paintings and carvings
demonstrate that Buddhism has become a folk religion here,
including magic and miracles and the ancient Korean spirits.
Dragons are carved surrounding columns. Taoist-type fairies hang
from high ceilings. Many of the best paintings are on the highest
parts of the walls or on the ceilings.

Buddhist temples are generally a complex of buildings, shrines,
and courtyards. Usually there is a gate decorated with images
representing the rulers of the four kingdoms in the four corners of
the universe. These rulers often are shown stamping out the
enemies of Buddhism. Statues of Buddha and *bodhisattvas* (beings
who have not yet entered nirvana) stand inside the main building.
Some buildings contain murals illustrating events in the life of
Buddha. There are more than seven thousand of these temples in
Korea, some as much as fourteen hundred years old and no two of
them identical.

*Seoul's east gate (left) and south gate (right)
are remnants of the wall that once surrounded the city.*

SEOUL

The first place most foreigners see in the Republic of Korea is
Seoul, its capital city. First-time visitors to this busy, modern
metropolis would never guess that it is nearly six hundred years
old, having been founded in 1394, a hundred years before
Columbus sailed to the New World.

At the end of the Korean War in 1953, Seoul was even more
devastated than Berlin was at the end of the prolonged bombing
of World War II. Because of this, most of the city buildings one
sees today are less than thirty years old.

Today Seoul has more than 10.5 million residents. In 1991 it was
estimated that Seoul was nearly the fourth largest city in the world—
quite a bit larger than New York or London. It is the governmental,
business, cultural, and tourism heart of South Korea.

Left: Toksukung Palace against Seoul's skyline. Right: A street in downtown Seoul

The city is surrounded by mountains and has two of its own within the city limits. People ride a cable car to the top of Namsan (South Mountain) or take the Skyway Drive over Pugak (North Mountain) to get an excellent view of the whole city.

The Han River, in the southern part of the city, divides the older section on the north bank from the newer southern residential sections.

A ten-mile (sixteen-kilometer) wall, built around Seoul in its early days, had nine gates that gave entrance to the city. Some ruins of the wall can be seen here and there on the mountainside, and five of the massive gates still exist.

Among the modern hotels, office buildings, and apartment complexes are the spectacular palaces, shrines, and monuments that tell the history of the city.

Left: Changdok Palace. Right: Kyongbok Palace complex

Five-hundred-year-old Kyongbok Palace is the largest of Seoul's royal residences. It is open to visitors every day, and Koreans by the thousands flock to see its splendors. Its gardens, courtyards, pools, and walkways contain many examples of Korean art from many centuries. A ten-story pagoda, a pavilion that is reflected in a circular moat, the National Museum, and the National Folk Museum are a few of the things people come to see.

Changdok Palace was built in 1405. Part of it is the residence of a few remaining members of the royal family. It is famous for its lovely 78-acre (31.6-hectare) Secret Garden, filled with pavilions, ponds, and streams.

At Chongmyo is the Royal Ancestral Shrine, which houses the ancestral tablets of the Yi dynasty kings and queens.

Yongin Family Land

Foreign visitors to Seoul especially enjoy visiting Korea House. This is a cultural center operated by the government where performances of traditional Korean music, court dances, mask dances, and folk dances are presented. The sets and costumes for the performances are gorgeous examples of the fine clothing and beautiful furnishings enjoyed by the upper classes in early years.

OUTSIDE SEOUL

South of Seoul are two places popular with Koreans and foreign visitors alike. Yongin Family Land, twenty miles (thirty-two kilometers) southeast of the city, is a combination zoo and amusement park, with an excellent art museum as well.

Traditional craftsman at work in the Korean Folk Village

Outside Suwon, directly south of Seoul, is Minsokchon, a Korean Folk Village. This is a wonderful, large, open-air, living history museum. Farmhouses typical of the Korean countryside, a market, and artisans' shops are among the buildings, all of which are authentically furnished with antiques and everyday household and farm implements. Visitors watch all sorts of handcrafts being produced: pottery, baskets, woven materials, brass vessels, and so on. Farmers are working the fields. A fortune-teller and a calligrapher work at their trades. And every day there is at least one celebration going on. It may be an old-style wedding, a kite-flying contest, or the ritual of a clattery farmers' band driving out evil spirits.

Left: Panmunjom, on the military demarcation line of the demilitarized zone. Right: A United Nations soldier watches the Korean People's Army headquarters from Freedom House, along the north-south border.

PANMUNJOM

Panmunjom, a thirty-five-mile (fifty-six-kilometer) bus ride north of Seoul, is the site of truce talks between the North Korean and Chinese negotiators and the United Nations Military Armistice Commission (MAC). A truce agreement was signed here in July 1953, but true peace has yet to come. An agreement to work toward negotiation of a permanent treaty was signed by North and South Korea in 1991 and ratified in 1992. In 1991 the two Koreas also agreed not to use force against each other. Another pact prohibited the use or possession of nuclear weapons. Negotiators from both sides of the demilitarized zone still meet for ongoing talks.

United Nations soldiers are still stationed on the south side of the

The harbor of Pusan

line, with North Korean sentries on the other. Tourists visiting Panmunjom report that is it a sobering experience.

In 1992 the United States and South Korea agreed there would be no further reduction in U.S. troops in Korea due to concerns over a nuclear weapons program in North Korea, who refused to allow inspection of possible sites. By 1994 the U.S. deployed Patriot antimissile batteries in South Korea because of North Korea's continued refusal of inspection. North and South Korea finally agreed to a meeting date in North Korea by late summer.

OTHER CITIES

Pusan, the second-largest city, major port and ocean gateway from Japan and the Western world, is primarily industrial. Hot mineral springs and good public beaches make it a popular resort. West of Pusan is the Hallyo Waterway, a maritime national park with picturesque rock formations and fishing villages, and Hydrofoil cruise boats that speed riders through the area.

The Hallyo Waterway includes 368 islands, 115 of which are inhabited.

Taegu has been known historically as a market city for the distribution of farm products from the southern region of the country. It is known for medicinal herbs and is the center of Korea's apple industry. Apples were introduced to Korea by an American missionary, and Korean-grown apples are famous throughout the Far East.

Today Taegu is an important industrial center, though most of its industries are small ones. It is located in a large bowl formed by surrounding mountains and is Korea's only major inland city. Taegu is also a college town. There are at least four universities and five colleges here.

Inchon is primarily a port and industrial city. In summer its beaches are crowded; they are close to Seoul and an easy escape from the city.

Kwangju is near Mount Chiri National Park. It has not as yet been visited a great deal by tourists, but serious students of Korean culture find many fascinating temples and other historic remains here.

Left: Kyongju's Buddha Triad, carved in the sixth century, is considered the earliest Silla period Buddha sculpture. The central figure, called the Buddha of the Western Paradise, is flanked by two bodhisattvas. Right: One of Cheju's grandfather images

The Kyongju valley, in a basin between Taegu and Pusan, is Korea's most outstanding historical treasure trove. The entire region has been called a "museum without walls," an "outdoor tourist museum," and "Korea's culture city."

The United Nations Educational, Scientific, and Cultural Organization (UNESCO) has named Kyongju one of the world's ten most important ancient cities and has included it in UNESCO's preservation program. It was the capital of Silla from 57 B.C., at the beginning of the Three Kingdoms period, to the end of unified Silla in A.D. 935.

There are more than 280 historical attractions in this area — temples, tombs, shrines, pagodas, monuments, and statues; the ruins of the Silla dynasty's most magnificent palace; the famous Chomsongdae Observatory; and the Kyongju National Museum.

All the great achievements of the ancient Silla culture are celebrated here in Kyongju each autumn in a three-day festival.

Pagoda at Bomun Lake near Kyongju

Cheju is the largest and best known of Korea's islands. It lies 60 miles (96.5 kilometers) southwest of the mainland, and its climate is subtropical, much milder than the rest of the country.

Chejudo means "Isle of the Gods" (*do* means "island"). Its scenery certainly is almost heavenly, with palm trees, brilliant flowers, a snowcapped mountain, caves, and wide, smooth beaches. Mount Halla National Park is on the island.

Because it is so remote from the rest of the country, Cheju has a subculture of its own. In fact the people of Cheju don't even think of Tangun as their founder; they speak of three spirits named Ko, Yang, and Pu as their earliest ancestors. In a park are three holes out of which these spirits are said to have emerged.

Cheju's trademark is a *harubang* ("grandfather image"), a crude sculpture carved from lava stone. The figure was considered a fertility symbol in the old days, and no doubt there are still believers in the Land of the Morning Calm.

MAP KEY

North Korea

Anak	G2
Anju	G2
Aoji-ri	E5
Chaeryong	G2
Changjin	F3
Changsong	F2
Changyon	G2
Chasong	F3
Chongjin	F4
Chongju	G2
Chongsong	E4
Chosan	F2
Haeju	G2
Hamhung	G3
Hamjong-ni	G2
Hapsu	F4
Hoeryong	E4
Hongwon	F3
Huichon	F3
Hungnam	G3
Hyesan	F4
Iwon	F4
Kaesong	H3
Kangdong	G3
Kanggye	F3
Kapsan	F4
Kilchu	F4
Kimchaek (Songjin)	F4
Koksan	G3
Korea Bay	G2
Kosong	G4
Kuumi-ni	G2
Kyoggi Bay	H2
Kyongsong	F4
Maengsan	G3
Manpo	F3
Munchon	G3
Musan	E4
Najin	E5
Nampo (Chinnampo)	G2
Ongjim	H2
Onsong	E4, 5
Paektu-san (mountain)	F4
Panmunjom	H3
Pokkye-ri	G3
Pukchong	F4
Puksubaek-san (mountain)	F3
Pungsan	F4
Puryong	E, F4
Pyongyang	G2
Sakchu	F2
Sariwon	G2
Sasu-ri	F3
Sinanju	G2
Sinhung	F3
Sinpo	F4
Sinuiju	F2
Sonchon	G2
Songnim (Kyomipo)	G2
Sunchon	G2, 3
Taeyu-dong	F2
Tanchon	F4
Tokchon	G3
Tongjoson Bay	G3, 4
Tumen (river)	E4
Uiju	F2
Unggi	E5
Wagal-bong (mountain)	F3
Wiwon	F3
Wonsan	G3
Yalu (river)	F2, 3
Yangdok	G3
Yongan	F4
Yonghung	G3

South Korea

Andong	H4
Ansong	H3
Asan Bay	H3
Chechon	H4
Cheju	J3
Cheju (island)	J3
Chiri-san (mountain)	I3
Chindo	I3
Chinhae	I4
Chinju	I4
Chochiwon	H3
Chonan	H3
Chongju	H3
Chonju	I3
Chorwon	G3
Chunchon	H3
Chungju	H3
Chungmu	H4
Haenam	I3
Halla-san (mountain)	J3
Hallim	J3
Hamyang	I3
Hwangsan	H4
Hyopchon	I4
Inchon	H3
Iri	I3
Kaeryong	H4
Kangnung	H4
Koje (island)	I4
Kongju	H3
Konyang	I3
Kum (river)	H3
Kumchon	H4
Kumhwa	G3
Kumsong	G3
Kunsan	I3
Kwangju	I3
Kyoggi Bay	H2, 3
Kyongju	I4
Masan	I4
Mokpo	I3
Munsan-ni	H3
Naju	I3
Nam (river)	H, I4
Namwon	I3
Pohang	H4
Posong	I3
Pukhan (river)	H3
Pusan	I4
Pyongchang	H4
Pyongtaek	H3
Samchok	H4
Samchonpo	I4
Sangju	H4
Seoul	H3
Sokcho	G4
Sorak-san (mountain)	G4
Sosan	H3
Sunchon	I3
Suwon	H3
Taebaek-sanmaek (mountains)	H4
Taegu	I4
Taejon	H3
Uijongbu	H3
Ulchin	H4
Ullung (island)	H5
Ulsan	I4
Wando	I3
Wonju	H3
Yangyang	G4
Yosu	I3

E

F

40°

NORTH KOREA

Sea

of

Japan

42°

38°

KOREA

G

36°

SOUTH KOREA

H

I

J

34°

32°

East

Huaite
(Kungchuling)
Chilin
(Kirin)
Lishu
Ssuping
Ssuping
 Itung
Shuangyang
Chiaoho
Kuanti
Tunghua
Wangching
Hunchun
Yungching
Arsenyev
MT. OBLACHNAYA
6086
C. NIZMENNYY
Olga
Hailung
Liaoyüan
Panshin
Kaiyüan
Huatien
(Chaoyang)
Tumen
Yenchi
Hunchun
Ussuriysk
Shkotevo
Artem
Partizansk
Chingyüan
Liuho
Huinan
Onsŏng
Hoeryŏng
Aji-ri
Vladivostok
Dunay
Vladimiro-Aleksandrovskoye
Hsinpin
Hunchiang
Linchiang
MT. PAEKTU
9003
Musan
Najin
Nakhodka
C. POVOROTNYY
Chienchang
Chian
Chesŏng
Manpo
Hyesan
Puryŏng-dong
Chŏngjin
Kyŏngsŏng
Peter The Great Bay
Kuantien
Kanggye
Changjin-ŭp
Kapsan
Pungsan
Yŏngan
Kilchu
Changsŏng
Wiwŏn
Chosan
Sakchu
MT. PUKSUBAEK
8275
Kimchaek
(Sŏngjin)
Iwŏn
Tanchŏn
Tantung
(Antung)
Uiju
Hŭichŏn
Pukchŏng
Sinpo
Sinŭiju
Teeyu-dong
Kŭm-ni
Hamhŭng
Sinhŭng
Sunchŏn
Tŏkchŏn
Hongwŏn
Hŭngnam
Maengsan
Sinanju
Anju
Yŏnghŭng
Korea
Bay
Sunchŏn
Yanggŏk
Munchŏn
Tongjosŏn Bay
Hamjong
Kangdong
Wŏnsan
Nampo
Songnim
Pyongyang
(Kyŏngju)
Koksan
Kosŏng
Chinnampo
Anak
Sariwŏn
Chaeryŏng
Pokkyeri
Changyŏn
Haeju
Kaesŏng
Kŭmhwa
Chŏrwŏn
Chŭnsŏng
Sokcho
Yangyang
Ongjin
Panmunjom
MT. SORAK
5602
Ŭijŏngbu
Chunchŏn
Kangnŭng
Kyonggi Bay
Inchon
Seoul
(Soul)
Suwŏn
Wŏnju
Samchŏk
Ansŏng
Chungju
Chechŏn
Ulchin
Yongtaek
Chŏnan
Hwangsan
Andong
ULLŬNG I.
TOK ISLANDS
(TAKE ISLANDS)
OEYŎN I.
Chochiwŏn
Chŏngju
Sangju
Yongil Bay
Taejŏn
Kaeryong
Kimchŏn
Pohang
Kunsan
Iri
Chŏnju
Taegu
Kyŏngju
Ulsan
Happyang
Namwŏn
MT. CHII
6283
Chinju
Masan
Chinhae
Pusan
Kwangju
Naju
Kumyang
Sunchŏn
Sachonpo
KŎJE I.
Mokpo
Pusong
Yosu
TSU ISLANDS
Izuhara
Chindo
Wando
Western
Korea
Strait
Eastern
Channel
Cheju
Strait
Cheju
Hallim
MT. HALLA
6390
CHEJU ISLAND
HIRADO I.
DOGO I.
Saigō
OKI ISLANDS
Kasumi
C. KYŌGA
Wakasa
Bay
HIGURA I.
NANATSU I.
Wajima
NOTO
PEN
NOTO I.
Nanao
Himi
Takaoka
Kanazawa
Komatsu
Fukui
Takayama
Gifu
Nagoya
Matsue
Tottori
Yonago
Kinosaki
Maizuru
Ogaki
Kuwana
Yokkaichi
Izumo
Tsuyama
Fukuchiyama
Kyōto
Kōbe
Osaka
Tsu
Matsusaka
Hamada
Masuda
MT. KAMMURI
4393
Fukuyama
Kurashiki
Okayama
Himeji
Akashi
Higashiōsaka
Wakayama
Yamaguchi
Iwakuni
Hiroshima
Kure
Onomichi
Tamano
Marugame
Takamatsu
Komatsushima
MT. HAKKEN
6284
Kumano Bay
Shimonoseki
Hōfu
Tokuyama
Nishihama
MT. TSURŪGI
6414
Gobō
Kitakyūshū
Ube
Nōgata
Iizuka
Nakatsu
Beppu
Matsuyama
Kōchi
Aki
Tanabe
Shingū
Fukuoka
Karatsu
Kurume
Oita
Ozu
Ino
Muroto
Kushimoto
O-SHIMA
Saga
MT. KUJU
5866
Uwajima
Kubokawa
C. MUROTO
Sasebo
Omuta
Nakamura
Shimabara
Saiki
Sukumo
Tosa-shimizu
Nagasaki
Kumamoto
Nobeoka
C. ASHIZURI
TORI I.
SHIMO I.
MT. KUNIMI
Amakusa
Katsushiro
Ushibuka
DANJO I.
Hitoyoshi
KYŪSHŪ
SHIKOKU
J H
A N
P
S
MT. HAKU
8865
Sabae
Ono
Osaka
Katsuyama
136°
134°
8

Statute Miles 50 0 50 100 150
Kilometers 50 0 50 100 200

℗ Copyright by Rand McNally & Co. R.L. 85-S-104

MINI-FACTS AT A GLANCE

GENERAL INFORMATION

Official Names: *North Korea* — Democratic People's Republic of Korea (DPRK); *South Korea* — Republic of Korea (ROK)

Capitals: *North Korea* — Pyongyang; *South Korea* — Seoul

Official Language: Korean. Hypothesized to be a member of the Altaic-Tungusic language family, Korean resembles Japanese in structure. Although unrelated to Chinese, fully half of Korean words come from Chinese due to Korea's long use of classical Chinese as its official court language. The native alphabet, *hangul,* was invented in the 1400s, and since the late 1800s has been used to create the modern Korean vernacular. South Koreans still use some Chinese characters; North Koreans do not.

Government: *North Korea* — The constitution of 1972 gives political power to the people through the Supreme People's Assembly, the legislature whose 687 members are elected every four years by popular vote. In practice, however, the country is ruled by the Korean Workers' party, the Communist party in North Korea. The Administration Council heads the government and is directed by the Central Peoples' Committee, all of whose members are high-ranking Communist party members.
South Korea — The president, head of both the state and the government, is elected by direct vote for one five-year term. The prime minister, who is appointed by the president, actually carries out the business of government. The president appoints the council of ministers. The National Assembly, a one-house legislature, has 299 members who serve four-year terms.

National Songs: *North Korea* — "*A chi mun bin na ra i gang san*" ("Shine Bright, O Dawn, on This Land So Fair"); *South Korea* — "*Aegug-ka*" ("National Anthem")

Flags: *North Korea* — Adopted in 1948, the flag features a wide red stripe with narrower blue stripes above and below and a red star (representing communism) in a white circle.
South Korea — The flag has a red and blue circle on a white background, representing the balance of opposites in the universe. In the four corners are trigrams (groups of three-line configurations) representing heaven, earth, fire, and water.

Money: The basic monetary unit in both North and South Korea is the won. The North Korean won is divided into one hundred jun. In March 1993, 2.15 North Korean won was equal to one U.S. dollar and 787 South Korean won were equal to one U.S. dollar.

Weights and Measures: Both North and South Korea use the metric system. Traditional measures are also common, such as the jungbo (one hectare) and the ri (3,927 m).

Population: *North Korea* — 23,494,000 (1994 estimate); *South Korea* — 45,019,000 (1994 estimate)

Major Cities:

North Korea (1990 estimates)
Pyongyang	2,650,000
Hamhung	800,000
Chongjin	792,000

South Korea (1990 census)
Seoul	10,627,790
Pusan	3,797,566
Taegu	2,228,834
Inchon	1,818,293

Religion: *North Korea* — The 1972 constitution states: "The people shall enjoy the freedom of religion as well as the freedom of anti-religious propaganda." Actually, the practice of religion is discouraged because it conflicts with the teachings of communism. There are three religious organizations — the Buddhist League, the Chondoist Society, and the Christians' League.

South Korea — Complete freedom of religion is permitted, with animism, Buddhism, Confucianism, Taoism, and Christianity as the major religions. Confucianism, not a religion in the strict sense but an ethical and moral system, is the dominant belief. Many people maintain a mixture of the various religions.

GEOGRAPHY

Highest Points: *North Korea* — Paektu Peak, 9,003 ft. (2,744 m); *South Korea* — Mount Halla, 6,398 ft. (1,950 m)

Lowest Points: Sea level, in both North and South Korea

Coastline: Korea's coastline measures 1,484 mi. (2,388 km)

Mountains: Mountains cover 80 percent of the land. The Kaema Plateau in the northeast has an average elevation of 3,300 ft. (1,006 m) above sea level. The Nangnimsan mountain range runs north and south through the middle of the Korean peninsula and divides the eastern and western slopes. The Khamgyong Mountains form a steep slope between the Kaema Plateau and the Sea of Japan. The Taebaeksan Mountains run in a north-south direction across the eastern coastline of South Korea.

Rivers: *North Korea*—The Yalu (known as the Amnok-kang) is the longest river, flowing southwest for 490 mi. (789 km) to Korea Bay. The Tumen River flows northeast for 324 mi. (521 km) to the Sea of Japan.

South Korea—The principal rivers—the Han, Kum, and Naktong—all have their sources in the Taebaeksan range and flow between the mountain ranges. The rivers are not much use for transportation, but are important for irrigation and electricity.

Climate: The Korean climate is similar to that of the northeastern United States. Seasonal winds called monsoons blow in from the south and the southeast during the summer, bringing hot, humid weather, and from the north and northwest during the winter, bringing cold weather.

Throughout Korea, July temperatures average between 70° F. (21° C) and 80° F. (27° C). Average January temperatures vary because the massive mountains protect the peninsula's east coast from the onslaught of the winter monsoons, and range from about 35° F. (2° C) in southeastern Korea to about -5° F. (-21° C) in parts of the northern mountains.

Heavy rainfall from June through August accounts for about half the yearly precipitation. Most of North Korea averages from 30 to 60 in. (76 to 150 cm) a year; most of South Korea receives from 30 to 50 in. (76 to 130 cm). One or two typhoons usually strike during July and August.

Greatest Distances:
>   *North Korea*—North to south—370 mi. (595 km)
>   East to west—320 mi. (515 km)
>
>   *South Korea*—North to south—300 mi. (480 km)
>   East to west—185 mi. (298 km)

Area: *North Korea*—47,077 sq. mi. (122,098 km²), including islands; *South Korea*—38,221 sq. mi. (98,992 km²), including islands; *Demilitarized Zone*—487 sq. mi. (1,262 km²)

NATURE

Trees: *North Korea*—Vegetation on the Kaema Plateau consists mainly of evergreens such as the Siberian fir, spruce, pine, and Korean cedar. Continuous deforestation during the Korean War left only a few patches of the original forests that covered the western lowlands.

South Korea—The long, hot summer is favorable for the development of extensive forests, which cover about 67 percent of the total land area and are made up of trees similar to those found in North America. Until recently trees were continuously cut down for fuel. Since the 1960s extensive reforestation programs have been fostered. A narrow belt along the southern coast has a subtropical broadleaf forest, but the remainder of the country is covered for the most part in coniferous trees. Fruit trees are plentiful, and Korean azaleas are prized throughout the world.

Fish: Shellfish and many kinds of saltwater fish are prevalent, including herring and anchovy. Carps and eels are important river fish. Fishing is an important industry, both for export and for domestic use.

Animals: Deforestation has had a negative effect on the animal population, and the number of deer, mountain antelopes, goats, tigers, leopards, and panthers has greatly decreased. These animals now confine themselves to remote forests.

Birds: Wild pigeons, herons, cranes, and waterfowl alight near the rice fields. There are several dozen native species and numerous types of migratory birds. Ironically, the demilitarized zone has become a preserve for migratory species.

EVERYDAY LIFE

Food: The Korean diet is based on rice, but also includes barley, fish, fruits such as apples, peaches, and pears, and vegetables such as beans and potatoes. One of the most popular dishes is *kimchi*, a highly spiced relish made from fermented cabbage, turnips, onions, red hot peppers, radishes, cucumbers, and other vegetables. With recent economic development beef has become a major protein source.

Housing: *North Korea*—Most North Koreans live in multiple-dwelling units or, in rural areas, in brick or clay houses with colorful tile or slate roofs. Almost all homes have electricity.
South Korea—In Seoul and other large cities there are many high-rise apartment buildings and modern houses. But in more rural areas most of the housing consists of traditional one-story dwellings made of thatch or homemade bricks. Most urban homes have electricity, and it is gradually being brought into rural homes as well.
In both North and South Korea little furniture is used. People usually sit on cushions on the floor.

Holidays:

January 1, New Year's Day
First full moon of the year, *Tongshin-Je*, community festivals offering thanksgiving for good crops
March 1, Independence Day honoring resistance to Japanese colonial rule in 1919
Early April (one hundred fifth day of the lunar year), *Hansik* (grave-visiting day)
April 5, Arbor Day
Early May (eighth day of the fourth lunar month), Buddha's birthday
May 1, May Day (North Korea only)
May 5, Children's Day
Early June (fifth day of fifth lunar month), *Tano* Day (prayers for good harvests)
June 6, Memorial Day

June 15, Farmers' Day

July 17, Constitution Day, marking founding of Republic of Korea (South Korea only)

August 15, Liberation Day, marking surrender of Japan to Allied forces

Early September (fifteenth day of eighth lunar month), *Chusok* (Korean Thankgiving Day)

October 1, Armed Forces Day

October 3, National Foundation Day (honoring founding of Choson at Pyongyang in 2333 B.C.)

October 9, *Hangul* Day (honoring invention of Korean alphabet)

October 24, United Nations Day

December 25, Christmas Day

Culture: *North Korea*—The development of the country has been the priority since the Korean War, and cultural activities have suffered somewhat. However, the government has made an effort to encourage arts that further nationalism and the Communist ideology. All writers, artists, musicians, and dancers are assigned to government institutions such as the National Orchestra, National Arts Theater, etc. Museums are sponsored by the government as well. There are more than a dozen, including the Korean Revolutionary Museum and the State Central Fine Arts Museum.

South Korea—Cultural life is pursued with more freedom. Western art has had a great influence; motion pictures and television, the most popular forms of entertainment, have developed rapidly since 1945. Korean art has been largely influenced by Chinese art as well as by the teachings of Buddhism and Confucianism.

The National Museum contains about eighty thousand artifacts of Korean culture, including many national treasures.

Korean architecture uses mostly wood and granite, and there are beautiful examples in old palaces, stone tombs, and Buddhist temples and pagodas.

The National Classic Music Institute (formerly the Prince Yi Conservatory) plays an important role in the preservation of folk music and graduates thirty musicians a year from its training center. The Korean National Symphony Orchestra and the Seoul Symphony Orchestra play concerts in both Seoul and Pusan.

Sports and Recreation: The 1988 Summer Olympics was held in South Korea. All the internationally popular sports are practiced—baseball, soccer, volleyball, tennis, table tennis, golf, archery, skating, skiing, wrestling, boxing, shooting, and swimming. A Korean style of wrestling called *ssirum* and the martial art of *taekwondo* are also popular.

Communication: *North Korea*—There are approximately ten newspapers, which are strictly controlled and censored by the Korean Central News Agency. The Communist party newspaper, *Nodong Sinmun (Workers' Daily News)*, has a circulation of 600,000. In 1989 there were 250,000 TV sets and 50,000 telephones in North Korea. Radio broadcasts reach all sections of the country and extend into the most rural areas.

South Korea — There are forty-eight daily newspapers, including six that are national and two that are in English. In 1990 there were 9 million TV sets in use, 45,000,000 radios, and 6,900,000 telephones. Although less overt than in North Korea, government control of the print and electronic media is very strict.

Transportation: *North Korea* — Railroads are the principal method of transportation. There are 3,054 miles (4,927 km) of track, 59 percent of which is electrified. The basic pattern is north to south. Because of the mountains there is only one east-west line. Most people own bicycles. More than 3,500 miles (5,633 km) of road are not paved. River transportation is important in moving agricultural products and minerals. Aviation is government owned and operated, as are all transportation systems. One or two flights a week go to Moscow, Khabarovsk, and Beijing. There are two domestic flight routes, from Pyongyang to Hamhung and to Chongjin.

South Korea — There is a rapidly growing highway system with more than 35,018 miles (56,481 km) of roads. Buses run between all major cities and bicycles are common. There are 3,859,000 passenger cars in use and more than 3,200 miles (5,150 km) of railroad track. Korean Airlines connects major cities with Hong Kong, Japan, Vietnam, Taiwan, and the United States.

Schools: *North Korea* — Eleven years of technical education is both compulsory and free. This includes one year of preschool education, four years of primary, and six years of secondary. Children must work during the summer from the fifth grade on. Students must have the approval of the Communist party to continue their education beyond the compulsory years. Those who are chosen to continue attend a two-year high school and a two-year general vocational school or a three- or four-year technical school. In 1985 there were 216 institutions of higher education, including one university.

South Korea — All children must complete elementary school (through grade six), and parents are required to pay some of the cost of a child's education. A student may go on to middle school (grades seven through nine) and then high school (grades ten through twelve). The cost of education increases after elementary school, yet about 80 percent of all those who are graduated from elementary school go on to college. Technical training is given at all educational levels. Students go to school five and one-half days a week. Qualified students may enter one of South Korea's over 250 universities, colleges, and junior colleges. Admission to colleges and universities is granted through competitive entrance examinations.

Health: *North Korea* — Medical care is free and each village has at least one clinic. There is a significant shortage of doctors and medicines, however, with 1 doctor per 370 persons and 1 hospital bed per 74 population.

South Korea — Medical conditions have been improving in recent years but are still inadequate. Medical personnel tend to leave the country to practice elsewhere, thus hampering the development of the medical system. As of 1992 there is one doctor per 1,077 persons and one bed per 429 population.

Welfare agencies are limited, but since the Korean War, United Nations agencies have been playing a significant role in improving living conditions.

ECONOMY AND INDUSTRY

North Korea:
Agricultural products: Rice, barley, corn, millet, wheat, potatoes, fruit
Manufacturing: Textiles, fertilizers, cement, chemicals, machinery, processed foods, shipbuilding
Minerals: Coal, graphite, lead, tungsten, zinc, manganese, iron, copper, gold
Fishing: Shellfish, anchovies, herring

South Korea:
Agricultural products: Rice, barley, wheat, beans, tobacco
Manufacturing: Electronics, shipbuilding, textiles, clothing, motor vehicles, petrochemical products, processed foods
Minerals: Tungsten, coal, graphite, iron ore, fluorite, salt
Fishing: Shellfish, anchovies, herring

IMPORTANT DATES

2333 B.C.—Korea founded by Tangun, according to ancient legend

108 B.C.—Chinese Han dynasty conquers northern part of Korea; Korea is ruled for fifty years as Chinese province

57 B.C.—Chinese control over Choson (Korea) collapses; three native kingdoms established—Koguryo, Paekche, and Silla. They last for seven hundred years.

A.D. 313—Korean forces drive out Chinese

372—*Taehak* (Great Learning), Korea's earliest school on record, established

647—Oldest astronomical observatory in the Far East built in Kyongju

660—Silla kingdom defeats other two Korean kingdoms, brings all Korea under its rule

668—Unified Silla kingdom period begins; period of culture, peace, prosperity, and foreign trade

682—First school for training of government workers, *Kukhak* (National School), established

918—Koryo dynasty begins when rebel leader Wang Kon forces Silla king to abdicate and assumes the throne

1200s—Entire body of Buddhist scripture is carved on wooden blocks to be printed; the 81,258 panels are called the *Tripitaka Koreana*

1392—General Yi Songgye establishes Yi (Choson) dynasty

1400s—Koreans invent such important devices as astronomical instruments, the spinning wheel, the sundial, the barometer, the rain gauge, the iron suspension bridge, and the ironclad warship. King Sejong invents the Korean alphabet.

1418-1450—King Sejong rules; golden age in Korean history

Late 1500s—Japanese under Toyotomi Hideyoshi invade Korea; allied Ming and Korean forces led by Admiral Yi Sunsin, using ironclad "turtle ships," repel Japanese troops

1592-1910—Korea's period of isolation, in which it has little contact with other countries; called the "Hermit Kingdom"

1630s—Chinese Manchu armies conquer Korea

1876—Korea signs treaty of friendship with Japan

1882—Korea and United States sign trade agreement

1883—Korea signs trade agreements with Great Britain and Germany

1894—China and Japan go to war over Korea; Japan is victorious; China gives up all claim to Korea

1904-5—Russo-Japanese war, after which Korea is a protectorate of Japan

1910—Japan formally annexes Korea; end of Yi dynasty

1919—Koreans stage unsuccessful marches against Japanese colonial rule

1943—U.S., China, and Great Britain sign Cairo Declaration pledging support for Korean independence

1945—Japan loses World War II; American and Russian forces enter Korea for surrender of Japanese troops there; joint US-USSR occupation divides Korea into two halves along the thirty-eighth parallel

1946—American and Russian negotiations over Korea's future break down

1948—Korea is divided into two nations; the Democratic People's Republic of Korea (North Korea) is established in the northern sector and the Republic of Korea (South Korea) in the southern sector; Syngman Rhee is elected president of South Korea

1950—North Korean forces invade South Korea; Korean War begins; United Nations forces come to South Korea's aid; China enters the war on North Korea's side and penetrates the south

1951—U.N. forces regain the thirty-eighth parallel

1953—Korean War cease-fire agreement is signed

1954—South Korea transfers some northern frontier districts by U.N. command

1956—U.S. and South Korea sign treaty of friendship, trade, and navigation

1961—Group of military officers overthrows Syngman Rhee's government

1963—Park Chung Hee becomes president of South Korea

1968—North Korea seizes U.S. intelligence ship *Pueblo,* accusing the ship of spying

1969—North Korea shoots down U.S. Navy plane off North Korea's coast

1971—Park Chung Hee introduces *Saemaul Undong* (New Community) movement

1972—Talks announced between North and South Korea, aimed at "peaceful unification"

1973—North Korea admitted to World Health Organization and granted observer status at U.N.

1976—Agreement between North Korea and U.N. establishes a joint security area on the north-south border, called the demilitarized zone

1979—South Korean President Park Chung Hee is assassinated; Prime Minister Choi Kyu Hah becomes acting head of state and is later elected president

1980—South Korea adopts new constitution; Choi resigns as president; Chun Doo Hwan is elected in his place; talks begin on north-south reunification, but North Korea breaks them off

1981—North Korea announces new reunification plans, but nothing comes of them

1984—North and South Korea agree to form a joint economic committee; North Korea sends aid to South Korean flood victims

1987—Death of student protestor detained by police sparks massive demonstrations in South Korea, threatening government of President Chun Doo Hwan

1988—1,200 student demonstrators arrested in South Korea during student march to truce village for meeting with counterparts in North Korea

1990—South Korean President Roh Tae Woo's party merges with two opposition parties to form the Democratic Liberal Party (DLP)

1991—North Korea and South Korea are admitted to the United Nations

1992—North and South Korean governments agree to reunite families previously separated by the Korean War; Kim Young Sam is elected South Korean president, the first non-military president in over 30 years

1993—North and South Korean governments agree on a restrictive reunification process that will work slowly to prevent monetary collapse; President Kim replaces cabinet members considered to have caused corruption in the government

1994—Working as an intermediary, former president Jimmy Carter attends talks between North and South Korea about North Korean weapons increase and refusal of inspection of sites; a 13-year-old from South Korea, Kim Yoon-Mi, becomes the youngest ever winter gold medalist when she wins the women's 3,000 meter relay at the 1994 Olympic Winter Games in Lillehammer, Norway

IMPORTANT PEOPLE

Chang Myun, president of South Korea from 1960 to 1961

Choi Kyu Hah, South Korean prime minister elected president in 1979 and resigned in 1980

Chongjo (reigned 1776-1800), enlightened king who helped slow the gradual decline of the Yi dynasty

Chun Doo Hwan, South Korean military officer elected president in 1980

Genghis Khan, Mongol conqueror whose forces occupied Korea in the thirteenth century

Kim Chong II, son of North Korean premier Kim Il Sung, will become president of North Korea upon his father's retirement or death

Kim Il Sung, premier of North Korea since its beginning in 1948

Kim Jae Kyu, head of South Korea's Central Intelligence Agency when he assassinated President Park Chung Hee in 1979

Kim Koo (1876-1949), leader of an anti-Communist group of Koreans who moved to China during the Japanese occupation

Kim Taesong, eighth-century Silla minister who built the cave temple of Sokkuram and Pulguksa temple

Kim Yushin, general who defeated the Paekche and Koguryo kingdoms and unified Silla in 668

123

Kojong, Korean king whose efforts kept Korea independent of Japan before the Russo-Japanese War of 1904-5; next-to-last king of the Yi dynasty

Kungye, rebel leader of the late Silla kingdom who tried to overthrow the government, but was defeated instead by Wang Kon

Kyonhwon, king of the Paekche kingdom who invaded Silla in 926 and killed the Silla ruler

Pak Hyokkose, legendary first king of the Silla kingdom

Park Chung Hee, general who helped overthrow South Korea's government in 1961, was elected president in 1963, and was assassinated in 1979

Syngman Rhee, first president of the Republic of Korea (South Korea), elected in 1948 and resigned in April 1960

Sejo, seventh Yi monarch, who seized the throne amidst political rivalry

Sejong (reigned 1418-50), enlightened king during Korea's Golden Age; inventor of *hangul*, the Korean alphabet

Sohn Jae Shik, South Korean minister in charge of reunification efforts with North Korea

Sondok, seventh-century Korean queen who built Chomsongdae, the oldest astronomical observatory in the Far East, and Punhwangsatap, the oldest pagoda of the Silla period

Sunjong (reigned to 1910), last king of the Yi dynasty

Taewongun (1820-98), regent who ruled for his son from 1864 to 1873 at the peak of Korea's isolation period

Tangun, legendary figure who is said to have founded Korea in 2333 B.C.

Wang Kon (877-943), rebel Korean general who overthrew the weakening Silla government in 935, renamed the kingdom Koryo, and established the Koryo dynasty

Wiman, military leader who took control of northwestern Korea in 194 B.C.

Yi Songgye, Korean general who drove out Mongol tribes in 1388, founded the Yi dynasty in 1392, and renamed the country Choson

Yi Sunsin, Korean admiral who invented ironclad "turtle ships" and repelled the Japanese naval attack under Toyotomi Hideyoshi in 1592

Yongjo (reigned 1724-76), enlightened king who helped slow the gradual decline of the Yi dynasty

INDEX

Page numbers that appear in boldface type indicate illustrations.

About the Author

Sylvia McNair was born in Korea, daughter of Methodist missionaries. A graduate of Oberlin College, she is the author of several travel books published by Rand McNally and Company and Fisher Travel Guides. Her articles on travel, education, and other subjects have appeared in numerous magazines. In addition to her free-lance work, she is a partner in an Evanston, Illinois, firm called Editorial/Research Service.

"This book is a labor of love in memory of my parents, Victor and Sylvia Wachs," says Ms. McNair. "They taught me to care about what happens throughout the world."

Ms. McNair has been active in various professional and community organizations. She was a founding member of Chicago Women in Publishing, has served on the national board of the Society of American Travel Writers, and was elected to two terms on a district school board. She has three sons, one daughter, and two grandsons.